off your rocker

Robert W. and Harriett Swedberg

Library of Congress
Catalog Card No. 75-5494

ISBN: 0-87069-126-0

Published in the United States of America by

WALLACE-HOMESTEAD BOOK COMPANY
Box BI
Des Moines, Iowa 50304

To Karen and Cheryl, who with patience,
learned to live with antiques.

CONTENTS

Chapter 1

ANTIQUE BACKGROUND

In a humanities research paper, our sixteen-year-old Cheryl lamented, "Since our births, my sister, Karen, and I have been surrounded by antiques. Our house is filled with them. Our cars are hauling trucks. Our vacations always tie in with them, and our lives seem to be run by these articles from the past." During their childhoods, our two girls shared a mutual passion—they hated antiques!

When the children were small, the family, en route home to the Midwest from an eastern trip, avoided the Pennsylvania Turnpike in order to visit tucked-away shops along more meandering and leisurely byways. Unfortunately, although many stops were made, every store was shut tightly. Finally, after a day of antique drought, a suitable motel was selected for the night. Cheryl's paper continued, "My sister, who was delightedly jumping on the bed, commented, 'There weren't any antique places open today, were there?' My mother replied, 'That's right, honey.' Then Karen took one huge hop, stopped bouncing, and very seriously said, 'Good! I prayed they'd all be closed, and they were!'"

Not even the most committed connoisseur can fight a child's faith.

The paper revealed that our two daughters, through exposure to heritage items, discovered new furniture becomes secondhand when it is placed in a home decor and usually depreciates accordingly. In contrast, antiques, which perhaps require some renovating and are bought for a fair price, can be expected to appreciate in value. Currently, financiers consider antiques one of the best investments with furniture a leader.

1

Today, thick slabs of sought-after woods are being replaced in cabinetmaking by veneers only 1/32" thick or less, glued over less desirable woods. Thieves sometimes steal walnut trees worth hundreds of dollars, because they aren't readily available any longer. Likewise, carelessness and blight have destroyed excellent varieties, so good cabinet wood is to be appreciated.

The girls also know that an "especially for me" decorating theme is possible through the creative placement of castoffs. Who, for example, among their acquaintances has a pie cupboard turned into a seen-at-a-glance housing unit for jeans and bulky sweaters or a dough box that is a treasure chest for browned, petal-shedding corsages, leafed-over letters, programs from past proms, or similar high school sentimentalities?

History ties in too. A portable family desk includes some features similar to the one Thomas Jefferson designed after his papers slithered and scattered, his ink spattered, and his quill pen splotched as he skidded and jolted over rutted roads in his carriage to attend the Second Continental Congress in 1776. It was some less distinguished traveler of the past who found the totable size of our lap desk compatible, its writing surface easily available, and its compartmentalized storage utilitarian. Today it is still functional, perhaps for Pop's jewelry or Mom's sewing.

As the sisters grew older and their appreciation of heirlooms deepened, they were eager to enter the workshop. Togetherness, as tightly clenched as a Chippendale ball and claw foot, can be achieved when a family goes creative or takes out frustration by turning a painted, weathered table into a conversation piece after hours of dirty, fumy, hard labor.

The girls can tell you that a depression Congress, for tariff purposes, decreed that antiques should be items created in 1830 or earlier. Actually, for our country, this original 1830 line of demarcation was not bad. Historically, the Industrial Revolution began as the 1700s terminated and the manufacture of materials in factories by machines slowly started to replace products crafted in the home by hand. It was not until the 1800s that this switch took on impetus. Roughly, then, the 1830 date distinguishes between handmade and machine manufactured articles. Later, a revised law stated that anything 100 years or older could qualify as an antique.

And then there's the dictionary that uses various terms, such as old; old fashioned; out-of-date; of a bygone style or time; and relic in its definition. The dictionary also concludes that furniture, silver, or other items made in a former period can be included. This permits pieces from the not-too-distant past to slip into America's heritage and gives credence to those who are not too exacting and declare that a generation's lapse is all that's required to classify articles as antiques. Then too, various sections of the country admire different old products, sometimes depending on when European settlers arrived in a given area. The senior antiques would tend to be found in the older settlements with juniors in later settlements, and today oak from the late 1800s and early 1900s rates A-plus with youthful scavengers. Another current trend indicates that native American Indian craftmanship is revered, appreciated, and respected.

Sources of Antiques

Treasure hunts are fun. Grandma's attic or Grandpa's barn, an uncle's garage or an aunt's basement may disclose discarded furniture that can be restored to useful attractiveness. A scarred chest with dribbles of paint, grubby picture frames, a decrepit rocker—all are worth retrieving if they are basically sound. Good woods, such as oak, pine, maple, butternut, mahogany, cherry, walnut or exotic rosewood, can be beautiful when refinished naturally. Base woods, such as dull gumwood or poplar with its greenish cast, may seem unpleasant to some but can always be stained. "Antiqued" articles are "in" at the present time, and this treatment could be used on woods that are not fine. So, exhaust the homestead sources first. You may turn up some family furnishings with a story. Then you can astound friends by exclaiming, "See our coffee table? It's really a trunk. Great-great Uncle Axel carried that with him during the Civil War." Or again, "Would you believe that little three-drawer chest had five coats of paint on it when we found it in Aunt Hazel's attic? We thought we'd never get it down to the natural walnut!"

If you have time to scrounge around, or if you like adventure, charity resale shops, secondhand stores, social and church agency stores, or flea markets may offer bargains. Household and rummage sales are another source for small, decorative additions. You may visit such places many times without finding any treasures, but how exciting it is the one time you discover a pine towel bar washstand selling for a few dollars or a set of oak chairs with machine pressed designs at a practically give-away price. It makes you want to hunt again. And there are stories of people who have gone to the dump and dug out valuables.

Estate sales sometimes feature a few articles at attractive prices. Also, auctions can provide diversion, but a few words of caution are necessary for a novice. (1) Arrive at the auction prior to the starting hour in order to inspect up-for-sale items. Purchases are usually "cash and final" and you want to know what you are getting. (2) When you find a desirable acquisition, appraise its value to you. Is it usable as is? Must it be refinished? Does it need repair work? Is it cracked or chipped? Once you establish its worth, determine not to exceed that amount. Dealers and collectors may want that same chest or table. Competition or excitement can cause you to overbid and climb above shop charges, so maintain your summit price. (3) If an amateur waits until the sale is progressing before he bids, he can determine the appropriate starting sum and how much the bid is generally raised each time. If you want something, remain calm and detached, or others may become interested. Hold your hand up high to signify a bid and to indicate your raise corresponds to the previous ones. If you offer a different jump, call out the amount.(4) Newcomers sometimes become confused and bid against themselves, upping their own price. Notice how the auctioneer recognizes a bidder so that you can avoid this fiasco. Also, families might become separated in the crowd and bid against each other when the article they have chosen is placed on the block. Be careful not to up your spouse's offer. (5) A wave or a nod can indicate a bid, so be careful how you acknowledge the presence of a friend. Otherwise, you may be the owner of an undesired purchase, such as a limping chair with missing slats.

Of course, antique shops seek to supply customers with pieces which are ready to go into a home immediately. However, patrons may request to see "furniture in the rough", the in-the-trade terminology for articles which need refinishing or repair. An amateur should hesitate to purchase a piece which would require a great deal of work, unless he knows how to use tools. If he must hire the job done, it may not be a bargain.

If you are looking for a certain article, some shops will try to find it for you. They may have a "wish book" and record the desires of customers by categories, even though they may not be able to secure a specific item. It might turn out to be too small, the wrong wood, too large, or somehow not exactly what was wanted. If it is a good salable object, a shop can buy on speculation, call the prospective purchaser, and, if it proves unacceptable, can keep it in stock.

On exploring expeditions, there are certain bits of equipment which might prove useful. These include: a pocket knife; a magnifying glass; a measuring tape; a magnet; a flashlight; and perhaps a pocketbook edition on antiques which includes a price list.

With the permission of the owner, the knife can be used to scrape a piece of furniture to see whether it is made of desirable wood. Insides and undersides can be examined also. Cabinetmakers in prior periods often used a combination of woods, since they stained or painted the surfaces to match anyway.

The magnifying glass helps find imperfections and chips or helps distinguish patent dates, signatures, or markings on metals, etchings, paintings, pottery or glassware. It also clarifies detail work. It may show when an identifying symbol has been filed off in order to make the piece appear older.

The measuring tape will tell you whether the table you have selected will fit in your dining area, and whether there's room to haul it in the trunk of your car. Furniture can look much smaller in a large store than in a home setting.

The magnet fills a detective's role, as it will adhere to iron and not to various other metals such as brass and copper. If a brass or copper wash (coating) has been applied over a ferrous base, the magnet will cling and announce this fact. Also, there may be a tattletale greenish cast (called verdigris) to the tarnish on brass, bronze or copper.

Flashlights help illuminate dark corners or in inspecting articles, but the small book with prices serves as a nebulous guide on what is a fair amount to pay. This is very general because different antiques are preferred in various sections of the country, and their cost is greater where they are most sought. Also, the market can change rapidly. For example, if a company reproduces a certain type of antique glass for the gift shop trade, people become suspicious of that pattern and may discontinue buying it. In contrast, the demand can climb upward rapidly. When leaded glass shades of the early 1900s suddenly became decorators' delights, their prices skyrocketed instantly. Round oak pedestal tables from the early decades of the 1900s once were almost outcasts, but now they sell for many times their original cost. In this manner, supply and demand can alter prices dramatically and drastically.

Signs of Age in Furniture

At a recent garage sale, the owner boasted about the excessive age of a petite rocker. His sales pitch went something like this, "That chair dates back about one hundred and fifty years. It belonged to an elderly neighbor who wanted my wife to have it. She was eighty-four at the time, and it had been her mother's who was eighty-one when she died years ago." This is the method many amateurs use in an attempt to verify age. They do not consider that the octogenarian could have purchased the rocking chair new at any time in her life and may even have received it as a gift in her last few years. Also, if this date line were correct, it would assume that mother and daughter did not exist concurrently because the seller is almost adding the ages of the neighbor and her mother to determine the antiquity of his wife's acquisition.

Or again, a young couple were just commencing their quest for antiques. They said to us, "You passed by our oldest possession without a comment. It's well over a hundred years old." We looked around and failed to see the article which prompted this ejaculation, and they had to point out their treasure to us. It was a turn-of-this-century oak buffet. "See," they said with deep respect, "the date is inscribed on the back, 1860." These digits were scrawled in large pencil-type letters and certainly did not match the style of the case piece, the wood it was made from, or its machine-crafted aspects. Although it was a good collectible item, we could not assure them that they had purchased a centenarian object.

What should the novice search for as he attempts to buy old furniture? Here are some stereotyped guidelines to assist the inexperienced, since it takes many combined clues to assess dates.

5

Drawer construction can be seen in this picture.
LEFT
Top: Machine pegs in a late 1800s walnut handkerchief box.
Middle: Machine made dovetails from a circa 1915 maple chest.
Bottom: Tiny handmade dovetails from a cherry commode of the mid-1800s.
RIGHT
Top: A series of small dovetails on a late 1700 "Chippendale" desk drawer.
Middle: A large single dovetail on a circa 1860 walnut handkerchief drawer.
Bottom: A glued and nailed construction from a patented 1898 oak spool cabinet
         drawer.

6

Period styles are only a very rough guide to age since furniture of the past is always being copied and revived. The Victorians, with their new machines, were eclectic as they imitated, mixed, and adapted freely the forms and motifs of previous periods. In spite of this, it does help to know and be able to recognize the common characteristics of the different eras.

The type of wood used helps. Museums or affluent collectors generally have acquired the colonial pieces from the 1600s and 1700s, or, when they are available, they are excessively priced. This leaves the 19th or early 20th century pieces available in antique shops. As a rough generalization, the following species were featured at certain times.

Mahogany—prior to and in the early 1800s

Walnut—middle and late 1800s

Oak—since you are not apt to find any authentic Jacobean articles from the 1600s, available oak pieces usually date from the late 1800s and early 1900s when mission and golden oak furnishings were in style.

Maple—generally will be from 1900 on. People boast about their beautiful cherry or mahogany furniture, but often they are fooled since it is maple with a red-hued stain.

Cherry—not abundant, but when used it dates from about 1850 or before. It is not an endurable hard wood and is of the fruitwood family.

Pine and poplar—used throughout the 1800s, often stained to resemble more expensive woods or sometimes painted. "Cottage Furniture" was painted and stencilled, and, when possible, such pieces should be preserved without refinishing as their quaint charm represents a specific period.

Examine your wood for signs of age. The width of wood on heritage tables and chests may be 18″ or more, with the entire top formed from one piece, or it can consist of a wide board with a small one to fill in. Today, a series of narrow boards are glued together to form tops. A leg or bedpost could be made from one hunk of wood in the old, not built up in layers as is the present practice.

Note the thickness. In aged articles, the wood may be over an inch thick.

Often a mixture of wood was used because the piece could be stained to match anyway.

Drawer construction shows age. Dovetails, a way of joining ends that resembles a dove's tail and interlocks somewhat as a jigsaw puzzle does, will not be quite perfect, each one identical, when they are handmade. Often the cabinetmaker scribed a line to show how deep to cut and a machine wouldn't require such a guide.

Notice whether there are rough chisel or plane marks on the outside bottom of the drawers which would indicate hand work.

Hardware such as handles, locks or escutcheons (keyhole outlines) offers clues. Sometimes these items are dated or have a name which can be traced, and various types were current during different periods. For example, keyholes from the 1700s and early 1800s might be inset brass outlines or wood inset in a diamond shape. Victorians might use round wooden or brass ones applied to the outside around the keyhole. Chippendale styles often feature bale handles. Hepplewhite used an oval decorative backplate and a bale. Victorians liked fruit, carved acorns, tear drops, and round wooden knobs. Late oak pieces often feature large fancy pressed brass handles with bales and elaborate applied escutcheons.

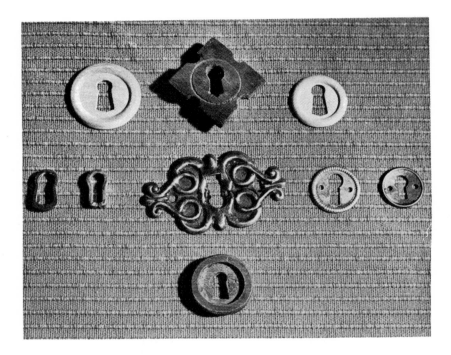

Some common escutcheons:

The wooden escutcheons illustrated in the top and bottom row are characteristic of the kinds used on chests, commodes, and desks of the mid to late 19th century. They were either glued to the surface or inset over the keyhole.

The large ornate brass plate in the center is typical of the kind used on pieces at the turn of the 20th century, particularly oak.

The different sized brass escutcheons pictured to the left in the center row can be found on furniture dating anywhere from the middle of the 18th century to the middle of the 19th. They are inset flush with the surface.

The round brass keyhole plates seen to the right in the center row are classical revivals and may be found on furniture of the Federal period.

Because reproductions are made of all kinds of escutcheons and craftsmen often change hardware, age cannot be determined solely by the type of keyhole coverings. They are only one of the many clues to furniture age.

Expect wear to show. Chair rungs may be scooped out from feet being placed on them. Legs can become slanted and worn down when the owner tilts back in chairs and rockers constantly utilized wear away and flatten. A housewife's broom often mars and scratches the base of tables or chests. Soft pine would have more nicks than hard woods.

Worm holes (really made by a beetle) do not necessarily indicate age. These can be faked, but real ones are irregular and twisty. Beware of powdered dust that would indicate that the larvae are still active.

Antiquers say that old furniture has its **own smell and feel.**

Nails might be square-ended, not inset into the wood, and not perfectly spaced. Ezekiel Reed of Massachusetts created a machine in 1786 to fashion nails.

Wooden pegs used in joining were not perfectly round.

Screws were used around 1689 and were made of iron or brass with blunt ends, not points. Modern sharp pointed screws date from the mid-nineteenth century. The head and grooves or spirals on early ones aren't perfectly even.

Corners on chairs would not be blocked.

Paint in the early days was homemade, often with a milk base, both because of its tendency to endure and its inexpensive availability, since people usually had cows plus extra milk. Red was a common color, although soft blue was utilized also. In the late 18th and early 19th century, it was possible to buy ingredients to create your own paint, but the premixed variety was not put on the market until 1867.

Remember, if something is painted and battered, it is not necessarily ancient. It is possible to apply layers of color and to distress wood with chains or pounding to create an illusion that an article has age. Recognizing real signs of age in furniture can be an assist to wise buying.

It's Going Around and You've Caught It

It isn't true. All antiquers can't be addlepated, odd, or off their rockers.

And yet, who else would trek 263 miles to another state with no other motive than to meet friends at the "Cow Bell Cafe," in a rural town they'd never heard of before, just to pry through the contents of a deserted, Civil War period, familial farm house attic, complete with its accumulated blackened dust, the current drone of wasps, and the wispy webs of very much alive spiders? Who else would be willing to delve into dank corners in a dark cellar to recover remnants missed by paper-shredding mice? That represents a quarantine case of antiquitis.

The frame house, built in 1863, is a restorer's delight, its weighty hand-hewn beams pegged together, its wide, wide floor boards solid yet somber with dark stain, its doors with their artificial graining and white porcelain knobs stoic and stanch. The round rocks in the basement must have been gathered at the edge of the nearby river and hauled by horse-drawn wagon to the home site. Besides all this, it contains attic to ˙ cellar, wall-to-wall antiques within.

As a bonus, the non-functioning barn, its log beams with much of the bark still clinging, has wrought hinges a foot long on its swaying doors. The light wood, all-of-a-piece, board on the feed bins creates envy. However, nothing, but nothing, could prompt the distaff side of this team (who, way back in childhood, pranced primly around all animal discards while her country cousins proceeded on through unheeding and unimpeded) to enter that dismal outbuilding with its rodents, lingering country odors, buzzing stingers, and dangling spiders. To climb over the heaped discarded furniture dumped inside was an additional hazard.

Soon tantalizing ejaculations erupted from those who were courageous enough to go in: "Hey, looky the size of the horn on that old Edison phonograph!" "This headboard resembles that on the one hundred year old youth bed our daughter slept in. Where's the rest?" Those were stimuli enough. Distaff was promptly inside, mounting a rusting stove, teetering across bed rails, and helping lug out the spindled side pieces and a couple of legs, literally dug by masculine hands from the hard packed earthen floor, until the crib had enough pieces to make it a whole.

Well, maybe, just maybe, antiquers are a mite loony after all, and, since you have acquired this book, you've probably caught odditis too so that you possess some decrepit article dug up from somewhere and you're not quite sure what to do with it. Then, why not explore with us the possibilities of its reincarnation as given in the next chapter?

Chapter 2

WHERE DO WE GO
FROM HERE?

Now that you have your in-the-rough antique table, chest, commode, chair, stand or desk, what are you going to do with it? There are various basic alternatives: (1) use it as it is; (2) revitalize it with an oil cleansing; (3) revive it with a water, oil and turpentine bath; or (4) remove the old finish and give it a complete face lifting. It is well to consider carefully these alternatives and the work each necessitates.

Use It as It Is

The first choice, use it as it is, is possible but not too practical unless your selection appeals to you and its finish is not objectionable. Still, some cleanup is necessary. Vacuum the entire piece inside and out. Don't neglect the back and underneath, particularly on case pieces such as chests and commodes. Wash the insides of the drawers with warm water and detergent, followed by a rinse with clean water and thorough drying with soft rags. Next, wax or oil the article. You have now done all you can to make your "as it is" piece usable in your home. If, however, your antique is too rough in this state and you want a more charming conversational attention getter, a more extensive cleanup is imperative.

Pieces with a dull, dead-looking appearance may show improvement when cleansed with oil. Connoisseurs believe that a bona fide antique should not be refinished. They feel that this decreases its value and detracts from its original state. They say, for example, that a mahogany Chippendale desk, circa 1780, which has retained its surface for around two hundred years might profit from a face cleansing but should not be tampered with otherwise. Cleaning with oil can offer a solution.

How To Clean Furniture with Oil

Turpentine, if desired or needed
Oil, such as lemon, boiled linseed, machine, or olive oil
Steel wool, grade 3/0 (very fine so that it feels soft to the touch
     and crumbles away readily when used)
Soft cotton cloths from old sheets, shirts, dresses, etc., with all
     the rough seams, buttons, zippers, and decorations removed.
     Lint producing or synthetic materials are not satisfactory.
A small container, such as a sauce dish
Paste wax, lemon oil, or a polish made of equal parts of boiled
     linseed oil and pure turpentine

Steps To Follow:

1. If a build-up of wax is present, immerse a clean cloth in turpentine, wring out, and, doing a small section at a time, give the antique a turpentine bath, rubbing vigorously. Dry with a clean cloth as you complete each section. This will remove the old wax.
2. Pour a small amount of oil into the container.
3. Dampen a piece of 3/0 steel wool in the oil.
4. Rub the dampened steel wool, firmly but not too heavily, over a section of the antique. Keep steel wool damp as you work.
5. Rub the oiled wood with a clean, dry piece of cloth to remove the oil and grimy deposits. When the cloth becomes dirty, take a fresh one.
6. Continue this process, doing a small area at a time, until the entire surface has been cleaned.
7. Polish using lemon oil or the linseed-turpentine polish, or wax with a paste wax. It is necessary to rub and dry the oils thoroughly with a clean cloth, thus removing any excess and preventing a greasy appearance.

When using this method, several additional tips are necessary. Avoid going across the grain with the steel wool, because this may cause slight scratches to develop. While, for the most part, the oil will prevent abrasions, be cautious anyway. You can determine the direction of the grain by careful inspection. The way the lines or dark-and-light character of the wood run indicate "with the grain." Going across this pattern in the fiber is called "cross grain."

12

Any of the above mentioned oils is all right to use, but if you wish a really pleasant smell, try lemon oil. The pure variety resembles the fruit in odor and is usually more expensive than lemon oil mixtures which contain harsh cleansing agents. These should be avoided. The results obtained from the use of this product are excellent. An oil not only polishes but also helps "feed" the wood and keeps it from drying out.

Before completing Step 7, inspect your surface, for you may find that it is necessary to repeat the oil cleansing treatment. More than this won't produce any better results, so you can stop there. When using this procedure, do only a small portion at a time, such as the entire top of a small trunk, chest, or commode, or the side sections of the same articles. On a generous-sized dining room table, it might be advisable to rub the leaves first and then the large center section. Be sure the dry cloths are clean, and don't be sparing in using fresh ones as necessary.

Brushing or vacuuming underneath, on the back, and inside is important in order to remove spider webs or an accumulation of dirt. These unseen portions should be washed and dried also.

Some furniture when created was painted or artificially grained and represents a certain style or period. If possible, this originality should be retained. Examples include country-made pieces of the 1700s in red milk-base paint; Pennsylvania German chests with their gay hearts, birds, and flowers arranged in neat panels; stencilled Hitchcock chairs first produced in the 1820s; and cottage furniture of the 1860s and 1870s.

If a clean-up job with oil will suffice, you will retain the authenticity of your piece and help preserve an historical record of the furnishings of a past generation. This is an admirable approach when feasible; however, some individuals prefer to completely strip the paint or graining and replace it with natural or stained tones, especially when the furniture has had ill usage. This is a personal decision, because you are going to live with your furnishings and you know what will be compatible with the decor you wish to establish.

The next method may be more beneficial in treating this specially painted furniture, but it is also excellent for cleaning other finishes as well.

Revive It with a Water, Oil, and Turpentine Bath

How To Clean Furniture by Washing

Turpentine
A detergent, such as Tide
Oil, such as lemon, boiled linseed, machine, or olive oil
Warm water
Two buckets—1 for washing and 1 for rinse water

Soft cotton cloths

Paste wax, lemon oil, or equal parts of boiled linseed oil and pure turpentine mixed

Steps To Follow:

1. When a build-up of wax is present, immerse a clean cloth in turpentine, wring out, and, vigorously rubbing a small section at a time, give the antique a turpentine bath. Dry with a clean cloth as you complete each section. This will remove the old wax.
2. Put a gallon of warm water in a bucket and add:
   a handful of detergent
   3 capfuls of turpentine (use the cap from the turpentine can)
   2 tablespoons of oil
3. Mix well.
4. Wet a piece of cotton cloth in the mixture and rub with vigor over a small section of the wood at a time. The cloth should be damp but not dripping.
5. Wring out a wet cloth, immersed in clean rinse water, and wipe over the part you have just washed.
6. Dry thoroughly with dry cloths.
7. Continue until entire piece is cleaned.
8. This procedure should be used with caution with veneered furniture. (See box.)
9. Wax with a good paste wax according to directions on the can or polish with lemon oil or the boiled linseed-turpentine mixture. Wipe thoroughly to remove any excess oil to prevent a greasy appearance.

Beware of cleaning products with silicone in them, as this penetrates into the wood and is almost impossible to remove if you should desire to refinish your antique completely. Furniture should be waxed or polished with oil once or twice a year. Too frequent applications tend to build up a grimy-slick appearance that detracts from the finish.

If these steps are completed with strength and diligence, you will be pleased to see how much of the old wax and dirt is removed and how the original finish comes to life, thus restoring beauty to the old woods.

Success in this water wash is based on the amount of firmness you use with the cleansing solution. A second washing (completed before terminating with number 9) may be necessary if some grime seems to remain. Remember, always dry your antique well; otherwise dark spots might develop.

CAUTION: See section on veneer and how to recognize it in Chapter 5.
Using this method on a veneered piece may lift the veneer, if the water is allowed to penetrate beneath the surface and loosen the glue. Wring out the cloth and you should have no problems. NEVER allow water to stand on the wood.

On case pieces (including desks, chests, and bureaus), this water bath is an excellent method to clean drawers that are musty and retain an unidentifiable odor. It is advisable to wash all unexposed surfaces. Not only does this improve the appearance, but it is also a sanitary precaution and helps eliminate clinging insects.

Sometimes examination of an article may reveal an alligatored finish. This is a scaly appearance similar to the back of an alligator which is caused by the finish separating over the years. Neither the oil or water methods will remove it. It is an age factor in your antique.

There is a way to remedy this with a special amalgamator which softens the finish and causes it to flow back together. Usually, however, it does not produce a satisfactory, lasting result. It may be better to do a complete paint or varnish removal job than to try this blending. Such a total rejuvenation is discussed in the third and fourth chapters.

The two courses previously mentioned have several advantages.

They can be used to retain an authentic, original finish to satisfy the purist's desire to keep an antique the way it was.

They are easier, quicker, less messy, and less expensive procedures to follow to make an old piece presentable than removing the finish. They eliminate the period of time, perhaps a week or more, that the various steps in refinishing require. Thus the item can be used almost immediately.

Three alternatives have been treated. Now it's up to you to decide whether you're going to say, "This has to be refinished." If that's your conclusion, the method to follow will be discussed in subsequent chapters. A good antique is worthy of laborious tender loving care, and the results will reveal the beauty of the natural wood to make you proud of your efforts.

Chapter 3

PAINT REMOVING
AND SANDING

Countless homemade formulas have been developed for removing paint and varnish. Although they may have met with success, you will find that commercial removers will serve your purpose. They have been scientifically developed, tested, and, when proven effective, have been put on the market. Selecting a brand must be your decision. Perhaps you know of someone who has achieved good results with a certain brand. Then give it a try. If you are dissatisfied, you can always experiment with other products until you find one that does the required job efficiently. Several suggestions, however, may prove beneficial. Don't buy a cheap type but insist on a quality name brand. The cost may be greater, but, in all probability, the result will be better. The remover should be spread on generously, so do not buy too small a quantity, especially when larger cans are proportionately less expensive.

Removers are usually liquid. Because they are powerful enough to take off aged finishes, certain precautions must be observed.

1. The fumes can be dangerous. Therefore, **adequate ventilation is essential.** Never work in a tightly enclosed space or tarry too long under some article such as a kneehole desk with three imprisoning sides. It is excellent to open a window or door and to stop at intervals to secure gulps of clean fresh air.

2. If you get some of the fluid on your skin or in your eyes, it can burn and must be washed off immediately.

3. Many of these mixtures are inflammable. Care must be taken not to smoke or to use them near a pilot light or unventilated heater. Some are

not to be placed in the sun because of their explosive possibilities. It is best to observe any instructions in this regard issued by the manufacturer.

4. The solution can also be very slippery when wet and can cause a worker to slide or fall.

Care and caution can help eliminate these dangers. Painted, stained, or varnished surfaces all react similarly to the application of remover, although paint takes longer to clean off than other finishes do. If you are attempting to remove a water base paint, buy a remover especially designed for this purpose.

There are two general kinds of removers on the market today. One requires water and the other does not. Both methods will be explained and you can select the one you prefer.

How To Remove Paint with a Water Wash Commercial Remover

CAUTION: See section on veneer and how to recognize it in Chapter 5. Do not use a water wash remover on veneered furniture because the liquid is apt to loosen the glue which attaches the veneer. Bubbles and raised spots result. On such surfaces, use a non-water type remover.

Paint remover
#2 steel wool
Hard bristle scrub brush
Knife, hacksaw blade, or any other sharp cutting tool, such as
    an Exacto knife or a chisel
Absorbent cloths, such as old towels
3″ nylon paint brush
Large coffee can or fruit can
Two buckets for water
Latex or rubber gloves
Old broom or long handled squeegee

Steps To Follow:
1. Protect your hands by wearing gloves.
2. Fill the coffee or fruit can about half full of remover.
3. Recover the remaining remover in its original can and set aside.
4. With a 3″ brush, flow—do not paint— a **heavy** coat of remover on the surface to be treated. A thin layer will not do the required work.
5. Allow to stand about 10 or 15 minutes before checking with the flat blade of a knife to see if the action has removed the finish to the wood. Be patient. Let the paint remover do the work for you. If the desired penetration has been achieved, proceed with the next step. If not, flow on another coat of remover over the entire piece. This is an additional coat on top of what is already there. Provide time for it to work as before.
6. Soak a piece of #2 steel wool in a bucket of water.

7. Rub vigorously on the furniture with the wet steel wool. Keep immersing it in water so it remains dripping wet and clean. Work with the grain of the wood from the bottom up to keep the moisture from dripping on the paint remover, because this will retard the process.

8. A knife, hacksaw blade, or scrub brush will help take the finish out of depressions, grooves, carvings, and other such places where it is built up heavier. Do this while the piece is still wet.

9. After all the remover has been rinsed off in this manner, go over the entire piece with clean steel wool and clean water. Sometimes hosing assists in this process.

10. Dry thoroughly with towels. This step is very important because black spots may occur if water is permitted to remain on the wood. Set the antique in a warm place (outside in the sun if the weather is not freezing) until it dries completely. Allow at least 48 hours for this process.

11. Sometimes when this method is followed, the glues are softened, but they will harden again as soon as the moisture evaporates. Be sure any loose joints on chairs are tight as the drying occurs. Apply a tourniquet or clamps when excessive looseness prevails on a piece and keep them in place as the article dries. (See Chapter 5.)

Before. A painted drop-leaf walnut table in its "as found" state.

18

12. Clean up the work space thoroughly with a squeegee or broom. Remover is slippery and can cause a bad fall if it is not scrubbed from the floor while it is still wet. Don't let it dry or you will have to scrape it off.
13. Left over portions of this type of paint remover should **not** be poured back into its container but should be kept in the coffee or fruit can in an enclosed metal cabinet. The brush may be left in the can to be reserved only for this purpose.
14. Most of the steel wool can be reused unless it has become clogged with paint. Rinse it in clear water, squeeze it out, and set it on newspaper to dry.
15. Wash the towels and gloves and hang them up to dry.

If, when you have completed these steps, you notice that a strip of finish remains on the surface, this is because you did not get an even distribution of remover on the piece, you missed this place entirely, or you did not rub hard enough with adequate pressure to remove the finish.

If this does happen, you will have to use remover on that whole section. again. Spot removing is never advisable. This area would be lighter in tone than the rest of the surface and runs, where the remover has dribbled down and continued to act, would become light streaks when dry.

After. A walnut table refinished to bring out the natural beauty of the wood.

The water wash remover has advantages over the other variety because the stripped surface is not only clean to the wood itself, but the pores on open grained species are free of old finish or stain. Also, this method is faster. Its disadvantage, if this is one, is that you need a place to work, such as a basement or a garage, where there is a drain and a cement floor. (Unfortunately, paint remover likes to gobble up tile surfaces.)

How much of an article should be stripped at one time? If possible, do the entire piece, because when it is done as a whole you will encounter fewer problems. When attacking an entire object, a helper is almost necessary. One handicap to doing the whole item is that some of the remover may begin to evaporate before you are ready to get at that section. You can solve this by dabbing on another layer over the first. If you simply can't accommodate the whole article at once, here are some guidelines to follow.

On small chests, desks, and commodes, remove the drawers and do them individually. Afterward, do the case.

On chairs, clean the leg section first, followed by the seat and the top. Keep the legs wet while you are doing the other parts. When you strip the upper section, go over the legs with steel wool and water to remove any drips.

On small tables, you can follow the procedure suggested for chairs.

On larger drop leaf tables, you will be dealing with a greater surface area. If possible, take off the top which is usually screwed into the side aprons. Make scribe marks on the underneath of the table top and on the inner section of the apron so you will know how to reassemble it. When the parts are separated, you can work with the top section and have no worry about remover spilling over. Then you can work with the legs. Do the underneath sides also on table tops and drop leaves.

On beds, do each end individually, followed by the rails.

On other furniture you will have to use your own discretion as to how to proceed. Always keep in mind to watch for and avoid any dripping, since it can cause lighter spots to occur. To counteract this, keep the completed area wet so any spilled remover won't act on it.

Remove the paint from the inside and outside of drawers. It's inevitable that, while you are cleaning off the finish from the face, drippings will run down the inside and along the sides. Actually, of all the parts, you want the inside, where you keep personal items, to be especially clean.

How To Paint Remove with a Non-Water Wash Commercial Remover

Paint remover
#2 steel wool
Putty knife
Knife, hacksaw blade, Exacto knife, chisel, or any sharp cutting
    instrument

3 large coffee or fruit cans, 1 for fresh remover, the second for
    the discarded used portion, and the third for turpentine
2″ or 3″ nylon paint brush
Newspapers
Latex or rubber gloves
Turpentine
Towels or clean cloths
Bucket of water to rinse gloves in

Steps To Follow:

1. Put on gloves.
2. Spread a generous layer of newspapers under the article to be
   paint removed.
3. Fill one coffee or fruit can half full of remover.
4. With your brush, flow—do not paint—a heavy coat of remover on
   the surface to be stripped. Do a small section at a time.
5. Permit this to stand for about 10 or 15 minutes, and then check with
   a knife by scraping to see if the remover has penetrated the finish to
   the wood itself. Be sure to let the remover do the work. Don't rush it. If
   the action is complete, proceed with the next step. If not, put on
   another application of remover over the existing coat so that there is a
   build-up and permit it to remain until a scraping test shows it has
   acted. Never permit remover to dry on the surface as this adds to the
   difficulty of stripping.

This round oak dining table has been stripped and sanded and is ready to have the desired finish applied.

21

Before. A pine carpenter's chest, as found.

6. Using a putty knife, scrape the surface and put the old remover plus finish into a clean coffee or fruit can. For places where a putty knife won't reach, employ a pad of steel wool immersed in turpentine, turning it over to a clean side as it picks up the old finish.

7. Before the remover dries out, take a knife and gently pry the old finish from crevices that the putty knife and steel wool missed. The build-up is usually heavy in such areas. A hacksaw blade works well in grooves and straight line depressions.

8. Now rub the antique vigorously with a piece of fresh steel wool soaked with turpentine. Keep the steel wool clean and saturated with turpentine. Next, with a dry piece of steel wool, rub the area to take off any moisture or remover remnants.

9. Wipe the article with a dry cloth (toweling is good). If any grooves have been missed, carefully dig out the grime with a knife.

10. Do not attempt to dab remover on missed areas on which the finish remains. This will cause that portion to become lighter than the rest.

11. If all the finish has not been removed, you will have to repeat the entire process. If you have followed directions implicitly, you should only have to complete the process one time.

12. Roll your newspapers up and dispose of them in an outside covered garbage can or in some other safe manner. Return any unused remover to its original can and clean your brush in turpentine.

13. Set your piece aside to dry. After 12 hours you can start the sanding step.

After. A naturally finished pine tool box.

Exercise caution with cutting tools, knives, hacksaw blades, or other such instruments so you don't scratch, gouge, or sliver the wood. If this does happen, you will have to do your best to sand out the damage when the piece is dry.

Sanding

Using Abrasive Paper

"Sandpaper" is a term inherited from past generations, and, although it is widely used in referring to papers which cut and smooth surfaces, it is not made today. Originally, fine particles of sand were utilized to make the product. Since it did not adequately smooth surfaces and caused fine scratching marks instead, other more effective types were developed. However, out of habit, both amateurs and professionals continue to refer to "sandpaper," even though they know it is a misnomer.

Today, the two abrasive papers most commonly employed in furniture work by both newcomers and experts are called garnet and aluminum oxide. Another is flint; for your purposes, this latter type should be avoided. The initial cost is less, but it wears out quickly and the economy factor is lost.

Abrasive papers come in large sheets measuring 9″ by 11″. They are usually marked on the back as to their grit, grade, weight, and type. The grit means the number of abrasive cutting edges per square inch which tells you that the higher number is the finer grit. Grade is the one digit followed by an 0, which is equivalent to a specific grit. In other words, when a person mentions 3/0, he is referring to 120 grit. Weight is recorded as A, C, D, or E and indicates the thickness. Generally speaking, A is extremely pliable and is reserved for very fine paper needed for finishing work. The type names the kind you are using, whether it be garnet, aluminum oxide, flint, or others.

The grits and grades and degree of fineness are listed in the following chart. You will satisfy most of your sanding needs by restricting yourself to these papers, although fineness does climb to 660 and coarseness descends to 20.

Abrasive Paper Classifications

	Grit	Grade
Very Fine	280	8/0
	240	7/0
	220	6/0
Fine	180	5/0
	150	4/0
	120	3/0
	100	2/0
Medium	80	1/0 or 0

Because most of your smoothing will be done manually, you should have available a block of wood about ¾″ thick and measuring 2½″ by 3½″ over which the abrasive paper can be placed. The block will enable you to sand smoothly and with an even pressure that you could not achieve if you simply manipulated a piece of paper in your hand. This size fits in your palm and can be gripped readily on the edges for firmness.

To provide paper of the size required for your sanding block, cut a standard 9″ by 11″ sheet into three equal parts lengthwise and then cut these three sheets in half. This will give you six usable small pieces with a maximum of sanding surface available. Also, they can be maneuvered in the hand without the wood insert to get in grooves and rounded surfaces which are difficult to reach.

After the old varnish or paint has been taken off the article of furniture you are working with, and all necessary repairs or filling of holes has been completed, rubbing it with sandpaper will smooth it to receive the new finish. Generally speaking, do not use anything coarser than 80. Most of the time you can begin with 100, move to 120, and complete the process with 220. For quality results, this step must be completed both thoroughly and carefully. One vital key to a fine end product is a competent sanding job.

Abrasive paper
2½" by 3½" wooden block, about ¾" thick
Cloths
Tack rag
Turpentine
Sanding mask (optional)
Orbital sander (optional)

Steps To Follow:
1. Check to see whether there are any marks, scratches, or remnants of paint or varnish on your piece. If so, use 80 paper to remove these to your satisfaction. Bear in mind that an antique will have many mars from age and usage and all these cannot or should not be obliterated. You will have to exercise personal judgment as to how many of the age marks should remain.
2. After all the imperfections have been eliminated to your approval, proceed to smooth the entire piece with 100 paper. Use the sanding block on flat surfaces and work the paper in your hand to take care of any hard-to-reach areas. Always sand with the grain of the wood. Cross-grain sanding will result in marks which will be difficult to remove.
3. Now smooth the entire area with one of the fine grade papers. Grit 120 is suggested, but any of the others will be satisfactory. Upon the completion of this stage you will notice and feel a smoothness appearing on the surface.
4. Number 220 is an excellent grit for completing this task, although any other very fine grade will produce the smoothness required for finishing.
5. There are many fine and very fine papers listed on the abrasive classification chart, and you do not have to follow each in succession. All that is necessary is to use one grit of fine followed terminally by very fine.
6. Vacuum the piece to remove the majority of the sanding dust. Cleanliness is essential if you want to effect an excellent finish.
7. With a tack rag, go over the complete piece carefully to remove any dust that the vacuum cleaner didn't pick up. This is a step that should never be eliminated. Other types of cloths are not satisfactory because they tend only to move the dust rather than to pick up the fine particles that adhere to a tack rag.
8. To be sure you have removed all sanding lines and imperfections, check your article by giving it a wet test by rubbing it with a cloth dampened in turpentine. With the moisture on the surface, you

can see readily any remaining defects. Also, this indicates the approximate color the finished piece will have. If any marks show up, it will be necessary to rub some more with 100 or 120 paper until they disappear. End, of course, with 220.

Some Additional Sanding Notes

An electric orbital sander is a useful tool if you do a lot of sanding, but for those of you who are only doing an occasional piece, hand sanding will produce just as effective a job.

A sanding mask is a good device to protect your nose and lungs from the wood dust that can saturate the air. It is almost a necessity when you use an electric sander.

Avoid belt or disc sanders because they are difficult to control and can create deep gouges, circular imperfections, and uneven surfaces.

Abrasive paper has long life if treated properly. Dust particles may clog the grits after extensive use, but these can be brushed out with a stiff-bristled brush such as a toothbrush. You shouldn't be too anxious to discard paper that may have a lot of life left.

Dowel sticks of various sizes, tongue depressors, or hacksaw blades are useful to wrap abrasive paper around to reach areas which aren't easily accessible by the other methods.

Too high a humidity may tend to curl your abrasive paper, so keep it in a dry area.

Although it is sometimes suggested that you start and finish with finer grades of paper on hardwoods (oak, hard maple, or walnut) than you do on softwoods (pine, poplar, soft maple, etc.), experience has proved that it isn't essential.

Veneer is applied in an extremely thin layer and must be sanded with great care. If mars are extensive, it may be impossible to get them out completely and the effort may cause you to sand through the veneer to expose the wood beneath. This must be avoided since this would disfigure the surface even more. It is better merely to smooth the imperfections but do not try to eradicate them completely. Be careful at the edges so you do not go through the veneer, since it tends to have thinned there with the ravages of time.

Chapter 4

HOW TO APPLY FINISH

Before. This is a battered, misused, mahogany veneered chest which needs some drawer adjustments, veneer replacement, and a complete refinishing job.

After. This cherry chest of drawers was in a state similar to the mahogany one until it was completely renovated.

There are a multitude of finishes that a person can choose from to complete his piece of furniture. However, for the best overall lasting results, and to achieve the durability desired, varnish is recommended for fine furniture. Of all the finishes, it is partially or fully resistant to water, alcohol, heat, and acid. Problems such as black rings or white ones are less likely to affect varnish than shellac or lacquer. Because of this, only the varnish finish will be discussed in detail. Brief notations on the other kinds will be included at the end of the chapter.

27

Varnish

Varnish can be applied by brush or by rag. Not too many workers use the rag method, because, by tradition, a brush is the required tool. However, if you have not tried using a cloth, you may be surprised and converted by the beautiful, easy, free results you can achieve. Be sure your work area is as clean and dustless as possible before you begin. Always stir varnish, but never shake it or bubbles will appear that will affect your finish. Remember, too, never to varnish in humid weather, because the moisture in the air will retard the drying.

How To Apply Varnish with a Cloth

A can of satin varnish
A small jar with a tight lid
Rags (from old sheets) about 12″ by 12″
A 2″ nylon brush
Newspapers
A clean stick or dowel rod to stir with
A tack rag

Steps To Follow:
1. Remove all dust from the article by wiping with a tack rag.
2. Spread newspapers on the floor beneath the article.
3. Stir the varnish and pour a small amount in a jar. Replace the lid tightly on the varnish can.
4. Cut a piece of cloth to the recommended size.

Before. Illustrated is a pine sled, in the rough, which needs some repair.

After. A refinished pine Swedish sled is shown.

5. Fold the cloth so it will fit into your hand and turn the jar over to get some varnish on the rag.
6. With the varnish-dampened rag, begin wiping over the surface of the piece, wetting the rag repeatedly as the varnish is worked into the wood. Complete one small area at a time.
7. On large flat areas, use circular motions to cover the surface. Rub in well.
8. Work from the top of the piece toward the bottom.
9. When each small section is coated, wipe with the grain to remove excess varnish. The article should have a shine but should not retain a damp layer of varnish.
10. Continue until all the piece has been varnished, including the under side of a table top and the leaves (to counteract warping tendencies) and the insides of drawers in case pieces.
11. In areas where the rag cannot reach (carvings, grooves, etc.), apply the varnish with the 2″ brush and then wipe it with the rag.
12. Your surface should be dry to the touch within ten minutes after you have completed this process.
13. Allow about six hours for drying before you apply the second coat.
14. Repeat this process until 5 or 6 coats have been built up.
15. Allow to dry thoroughly and your piece will then be ready for rubbing out. (See end of chapter.)

Wiping the varnish on with a rag has many advantages over the brush method. For one, the surface is dry to the touch quickly, which means that dust and dirt particles will not adhere to it and cause problems that might require sanding in order to smooth them. Another advantage is that you will not have runs (where the varnish dribbles down the piece and causes a line of heavier finish) because coats are not thick and wet. Furthermore, the wiping method enables you to work the finish into the wood rather than achieving a surface application, and, since the coats are lighter, they do not give a heavy look to the completed pieces of furniture. Actually, the finish becomes a part of the wood itself. It is not necessary, either, to sand between coats (as it often is with the brush method), because the drying time is so rapid little, if any, dust can stick to the surface.

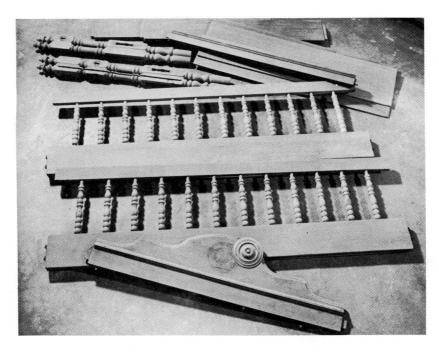

Before. The disassembled parts of a walnut baby bed have been stripped and sanded and are ready to be put back together again.

Can of satin varnish
3″ nylon brush (or you may buy a special varnish brush)
Newspapers
Small can
Tack rag
Clean stick or dowel rod to stir with

Steps To Follow:
1. Remove all dust from the article by wiping with a tack rag.
2. Spread newspapers on the floor beneath the piece.
3. Stir the varnish with a stick, and then pour a small amount into a can. Replace the lid tightly on the original can. A newspaper covering will prevent splatters while the cover is tapped in place with a hammer.
4. Dip the brush into the varnish and then work it back and forth on clean newspapers to force the varnish equally throughout the bristles.

After. A walnut youth bed, a counterpart of the unfinished baby bed, has been finished with six coats of varnish applied with a cloth.

5. Dip the brush into the can of varnish, but never more than halfway into the bristles. Before applying, wipe the brush lightly against the edge of the container to release any excess liquid.
6. As you work, hold the brush so the finger and thumb rest on the upper part of the ferrule (the metal section that holds the bristles).
7. Now lay the varnish on the surface, doing small sections at a time, working from the center toward the edge. Use short, quick strokes. Flow it on and brush very little to avoid leaving brush marks. This is done on horizontal surfaces.

Before. A painted pine cupboard in need of restoration.

8. Brush only to pick up excess varnish. Then hold the brush straight up and down and lightly flick over the surface with the tip to secure an even result.

9. On vertical pieces, use short strokes working back and forth across the surface. Brush half way down and then half way up, so that the brush strokes are picked up at the midway point. Work small areas until the whole section is completed.

10. On portions such as the legs of tables or chairs, brush around the turning but apply straight down on the plain sections of the legs.

After. A refinished pine cupboard which needed a great deal of work.

33

11. Do the underneath of table leaves, table tops, or other flat surfaces that may warp if they are not finished. Give the insides of drawers a coat also.
12. When you have covered the entire piece of furniture, inspect carefully for any runs. Use the tip of the brush to stroke them smooth.
13. Allow the surface to dry thoroughly before applying the next coat. Sand lightly with 6/0 sandpaper to smooth the surface between coats. Dust with a tack rag.
14. Proceed with any succeeding coats in the manner described above.

Rubbing Out

When you have applied enough coats to satisfy your taste, you are ready for the final rubbing out. Proceed by lightly sanding the piece with 6/0 sandpaper to obtain a smooth satin feel. Then rub the entire piece with 3/0 steel wool so you dull the surface and blend the finish. Vacuum and tack rag the article to remove the dust. Wipe vigorously with a soft cloth to bring out the desired sheen. You may, if you choose, wax the piece with a quality paste wax. Your acquisition is now ready for placement in your home.

Other Possible Finishes

Shellac

Shellac mixed equally with shellac thinner or denatured alcohol is quick drying and is a rapid way to finish objects that do not receive much wear or handling, such as picture frames, novelty wooden wall decorations, or other small objects. Apply it quickly with even brush strokes. Do not attempt to go back over any of it as it dries so rapidly that streaks can develop when an attempt to "touch up" is made. This finish is not as hard and lasting as varnish is. Black rings occur quickly when moisture is allowed to stand, and, on pieces that come in contact with the body, black marks can result where perspiration touches the finish.

Wax Finish

It is inadvisable to apply paste wax on bare wood because of the difficulty in removing it if you decide you prefer a different finish. Wax alone is not adequate because accumulations of grime can become intermingled with it, and a dusty, dirty appearance may soon result. However, if you elect to use wax, apply it according to the manufacturer's directions.

Shoe Polish Finish

Colored shoe polish, which is a wax, can be used to finish small articles of furniture, picture frames, or other items which do not receive much wear or handling. All old finish must be removed, and the piece must be sanded smooth before the polish is applied with a rag or shoe dabbing brush. You may put natural on any wood, but if you wish to color the piece a deeper tone, use a darker shade. Three or four applications (you be the judge) may be required, and it is necessary to rub the surface briskly with a clean cloth after each one. When the proper sheen is achieved, you can stop. Do not use the spray-on variety of polish, but always choose the paste wax type. This method will not give light woods the deep tone that stains will, so you might experiment on scrap pieces of wood first in order to check the end color you will achieve. This is a quick method, but, like paste wax over bare wood, dirt will become attached to the piece and eventually a grimy appearance may result. This can be remedied by cleaning with turpentine and then reapplying the polish.

Chapter 5

EASY REPAIRS THE AMATEUR CAN DO

Gluing Tips

Clamps

Quality liquid furniture glue, such as white or hide.

Bucket of water

Tools, such as a file, chisel, Exacto knife

Small wooden blocks about 2½″ x 1½″ and ¼″ thick. Have enough to insert at each point where a clamp comes into contact with the piece of furniture

Wax paper

Wet and dry cloths

Masking tape

Pencil or pen

Tongue depressors, ice cream sucker sticks, or something flat for applying the glue

Steps To Follow:

1. When you disassemble any piece of furniture with the intention of regluing it, always mark the sections so that they can be returned to their original positions. This is especially true of chairs. Removed rungs should be replaced in the exact location as they were originally. Mark all parts, before disassembling, with masking tape to indicate position and place. Letter matching socket and inset "A" "A", "B" "B", etc., indicate the upper side of rungs, and add any other vital reminders to the tape.

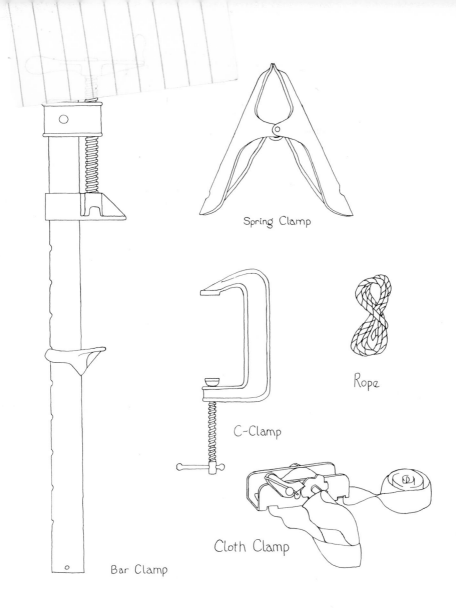

Spring Clamp

C-Clamp

Rope

Cloth Clamp

Bar Clamp

2. An essential aspect in gluing is that the joints which are to meet must be clean and fit properly. The old glue may be loosened with water because most glues are soluble in water. While it is wet it can be scraped away more easily than when it is dry. Use files, chisels, Exacto knives, or steel wool (#2) saturated in water for the removal process. Dry with a cloth.

37

3. On the ends of chair rungs, where they fit into sockets, files are good to remove hardened glue and to rough up the surface in order to permit more of the fresh glue to seep in to make a better joint. A rat-tail file and chisels are useful in clearing the glue from the sockets.
4. After all of the joints have been cleaned, reassemble the parts before adding glue to check if all sections fit securely. This is called a "dry run" because it enables you to see where more cleaning must be done in order to achieve a good fit.
5. If the "dry run" shows that all sections fit properly, you are ready for the application of glue.
6. An excessive amount of glue cannot compensate for the space in an improper connection in a chair socket. The remedy for this is the insertion of small wooden wedges to insure a proper fit.
7. Apply an even amount of glue on each section. Wait awhile to allow them to become tacky.
8. Reassemble the parts when the glue is ready, and apply clamps to insure a tight fit. If bar clamps are used, always place small blocks of wood between the clamp's points of contact and the wood to prevent impressions caused by pressure.
9. Wax paper placed on the surface under the blocks will prevent them from sticking if any glue oozes out. Apply masking tape over holes and around the joints to eliminate running glue.
10. Be sure all surfaces are even. Chairs and tables must sit flat on the floor and not wobble. If there is any doubt, remove clamps and start again.
11. Always wipe any excess glue off with a wet cloth and then a dry one. If the glue hardens on the exposed portion of the furniture, stains will not penetrate, nor will varnish adhere and look well. An unsightly appearance will be the result.
12. If you do not own clamps, it is sometimes possible to bind with a rope, twisting and bracing it tightly with a stick in a tourniquet fashion. Always pad points of contact with the furniture to prevent burns. At times, weights, such as cement blocks put over a sheet of wax paper, can be used to hold flat surfaces together until the glue dries.
13. If one joint of a seat is insecure, the entire chair may soon wobble as each joint seems to react to the others. Therefore, it is best to reglue immediately when a weak connection is noted.

WARNING: Some people make the mistake of squirting glue into joints that have not been cleaned of the old adhering agent. This will hold temporarily but will soon pull loose again. All old glue should be soaked and pried away before new is added.

If a socket on a chair is enlarged, small wooden wedges inserted in it will help assure a snug fit.

A spring clamp can be used to apply escutcheons to drawer fronts. The block prevents damage where the clamp exerts pressure.

Removing Warps

Warping is a common problem that faces antiquers and is especially common in table tops and leaves. Fortunately, however, any solid wood that warps will unwarp. The damage, characterized by an upward curve, occurred in the first place because the underneath side of the wood was not protected with a finish, and more dampness was absorbed there than on the top surface. Consequently, when you correct the situation, you are simply equalizing the amount of moisture in the two sides. Always remember when you are working on furniture to finish the under sections too, to prevent such damage.

As a first step, all of the old finish must be taken off. Then, detach the afflicted top or leaf. Warm, sunny weather is the ideal time to do this job. Place the warped section on moist grass (wet with a hose or by rain or dew), with the concave side, which resembles the inner part of a circle, down. Let the sun's rays pull the board back into place. When the warp has been removed, take the piece inside to dry. Clamp with boards so the shape is retained, or immediately attach the piece back in its original position. If the sun is not available, you may try some artificial means of applying heat, such as a stove, portable heater, or a radiator. The heat should be attacking the convex side (the outer part of a circle), and moisture or damp cloths should be on the concave slope. You can also saturate the concave curve with water. Watch what you're doing, as the wood can also bow the other way if too much dampness is permitted to penetrate.

Repairing Splits Where Wood Has Separated

Where wood has separated and a split has occurred because of drying out, or where the original joint has loosened and parted company, the best procedure is to remove that section from the piece, clean the joint, glue it, and clamp it back in place. If it is not possible to extract the section, another remedy is conceivable. Secure wood of the same species and cut a piece the length of the split. Taper the end that is to be put in the split, and apply glue in the crack and on the insert piece. Tap it into place with a hammer, using a board on top of it to keep the blows from denting the wood surface. When the glue dries, chisel any excess wood off and then sand until smooth, beginning with a coarse paper and finishing with a finer grade.

Removing Dents

Dents in furniture can be wholly or partially removed by using an iron and steaming them so they come up flush with the surface. This is possible only when none of the wood fibers have been removed, such as in a cut. Lay a cloth, thoroughly soaked with water, on the afflicted part to provide moisture and set a hot iron on it. Repeat the process until you can see the wood fibers expanding and rising. Of course, all finish must be removed in order to allow the dampness to penetrate the wood fibers.

When moisture spreads over the surrounding area, wipe it off with a dry cloth. Soft woods respond more easily to this process than do hard woods. Dents in maple are extremely difficult, if not impossible, to remove. It is always advisable to try this cure first before trying filler, because the end result will be more natural looking. This remedy applies to solid woods, not veneered surfaces.

Techniques with Veneer

To veneer means to cover a base wood with a finer variety which has decorative coloring or markings. Fragile woods can be strengthened by gluing them to another surface in this manner. It helps make beautiful patterns available in larger quantities because 32 sheets of veneer can be cut from an inch of wood to supply the American furniture market.

Repairing Bubbles in Veneer

When a small section of veneer becomes loose, raises, and looks almost like a bubble, take a razor blade and slit it in pie-shaped wedges. This is a delicate operation and should be done with care. Take a flat stick, such as a tongue depressor, and with it apply hide or white glue to the surface and to the underside of the upraised veneer. Press down. Wipe off excess glue with a damp and then a dry cloth. Place wax paper over the surface, and weight it down to keep the piece securely in place until the glue dries. Allow 24 hours for this.

Replacing Veneer

It is better to let a qualified craftsman repair badly damaged veneer than to attempt extensive work yourself. However, when a small section is missing, you can cut away jagged edges on a slant, and insert a piece that matches as well as possible. Follow the gluing procedures stated previously under "Repairing Bubbles." If you use clamps instead of weights, be sure to place wooden blocks under the pressure points to prevent damage to the surface.

Removing Veneer

You may have a need to remove old veneer from a piece. This can be accomplished as follows: First, strip all the old finish off. Next, get an electric iron, a putty knife, can with some water in it, and some rags. Wet the cloths in the water and fold them; then place them on the veneered surface and set the heated iron flat, without moving it, over the small section which they cover. The heat and moisture will loosen the glue, and the putty knife can be used to strip off the veneer. Care should be taken not to gouge the wood beneath by trying to remove too large a portion at a time or by forcing up parts where the steam has not penetrated. You can save the removed veneer, because it may come in handy in future repair work. Often, the wood beneath it is pine, and there are people who have stripped the veneer off an entire piece of furniture to expose this wood. They think that they are getting the old appearance, but this is not true because the style is not that of a pine primitive.

Filling Holes with Wax Sticks

Before any finish is applied, a simple way to correct holes in furniture is to use wax sticks which can be melted and mixed in a jar lid heated over an alcohol burner. Since wax is highly combustible and can flare up and burn readily, only a slow, low heat is used. Mix and melt crayons or other colored wax until you achieve a tone which blends with the wood in the piece of furniture. Since dried tones are different from wet ones, you should let your sample mixture harden to see if the dried color matches the mother piece. When it does, remelt the wax and work the molten material into the depression with a flat instrument such as a knife. After it hardens, scrape away any excess with a razor blade until the filler is even with the existing surface. Seal the entire section with a combination of half shellac and half denatured alcohol or shellac thinner. After this protective coating dries, you may apply the finish you desire without fear that the wax will bleed through.

A chisel is a useful tool in cleaning chair joints.

A file can help clean chair stretchers. Notice that each piece is marked so that it can be returned to its original position.

Filling Holes with Wood Dough

Wood dough is a material which is easy for the inexperienced furniture repairman to work with. It can fill holes, small cracks, and other minor imperfections if a great deal of the basic wood is not missing. These doughs may be purchased in various tones, such as mahogany, walnut, pine, oak, cedar, or others, but you will find that intermixing is necessary to secure a match for the wood you are working with. For example, walnut and mahogany combine well to emulate cherry, walnut and mahogany. Apply with a knife and sand when dry to acquire a smooth surface. If the color does not match to your satisfaction, you may try to make it more realistic by stroking oil colors mixed with varnish on the filled area with an artist's brush.

Filling Holes with Glue and Wood Dust

Save some of the wood dust from sanding your antique, and mix it with glue to make a filler to match the piece you are restoring. Since this wood dust does come from the furniture itself, you should achieve a fairly close blending. Follow the procedures listed under filling holes with wood dough.

43

Repairing Drawer Slides or Drawer Runners

After years of service, much wear will be noticeable on the bottom edges so that drawers no longer run smoothly along their guides (the narrow wooden runners inside the chest). This can be remedied in either of two ways, or perhaps both. Add strips to the bottom of the worn sections of the drawers to make them even once again. Smooth the worn portion first with sandpaper, dust, and glue on the strips. Use clamps to hold them securely until they dry (about 24 hours). Also, you can use wood dough to fill in the depressions on the drawer guides where much wear has occurred. Permit it to dry and sand smooth to complete the job. These two procedures will give new life to old drawers and will help them function with efficiency.

Silicone Grease Stick

Silicone grease sticks have two important functions in furniture work. First, they help to make drawers slide with ease. Rub the silicone on the bottom of the slides and the inside runners, and work the drawers back and forth until they move smoothly. Secondly, they can be applied to the threads to make screws enter wood more easily.

Inserting New Screws

Sometimes it may be necessary to use screws to attach a piece to your article of furniture. When doing this, always drill a pilot hole for the screw, enlarging the end because it is larger. Grease the threads with silicone and screw in place. Do not attempt to insert nails indiscriminately since they will not hold and can cause damage.

Loose Screws

Oftentimes, screws may be loose in your piece, particularly beneath the table top where they are inserted to secure the top to the apron. If tightening them will not make them hold, then you will have to remove them and proceed in either of two ways. (1) Put slivers of wood in the holes (from a match stick or old wood around your home) and reinsert the screw. (2) Fill the hole with wood dough. Put silicone grease on the screw threads and insert the screw. When the wood dough tightens, the screw can be extracted easily, if necessary, because of the grease on the threads.

Removing White and Black Rings on Furniture

White rings are caused by moisture that has penetrated the finish but has not reached the wood itself. These spots or rings can be removed by moistening a piece of 3/0 steel wool in oil, such as mineral, lemon, or boiled linseed, and rubbing briskly over them until they disappear. Once white areas have been removed, follow the same process on the entire surface to blend the tone of the wood finish.

Black rings occur when moisture has penetrated through the finish and into the wood itself. The cure for this is to remove the finish and bleach the entire section with oxalic acid. See the instructions which follow.

Bleaching with Oxalic Acid Crystals [or Powder]

Dissolve the crystals or powder in one pint of hot water until the water is saturated or will hold no more of the acid. Brush this mixture over the affected area, and allow it to dry until crystals form, or until you see that the discoloration has disappeared. Wash with about one pint of clean water to which 4 or 5 capfuls of ammonia or white vinegar have been added. This neutralizes the oxalic acid and stops any further bleaching action. Finish by washing the surface with clean water. Allow at least 24 hours drying time before continuing to work on the piece. NEVER spot bleach because you will end up with a portion which will be lighter in color than the surrounding wood.

> CAUTION: Oxalic acid is a poison and should be stored with care, especially around children. When using it, have plenty of ventilation. Beware of fumes. Wash off immediately if some gets on the skin or in the eyes.

Revitalizing Washed-Out Wood Tones

Often when the finish has been removed from woods, a gray, washed-out tone is apparent. The hard, long way to remove this is to sand it out. That requires hours of effort, and on maple, particularly, it is most difficult, especially when you are working on a piece that has turnings. Instead, try washing the article with full strength bleach, letting it dry and sanding it lightly.

Removing Filler Left in the Grain after Stripping

Much of the old furniture constructed from open-grained woods, such as walnut or mahogany, was covered with a paste filler which was absorbed in the pores in order to give the surface a smooth appearance when it was finished. Occasionally some remains following stripping. It is white in color and can be seen when a new clear finish is applied. However, if you are staining your piece of furniture, this white substance will take on color and will not show. If you finish your piece naturally (which many antiquers feel is the best approach with fine woods), you will want to remove this unsightly filler. The following method has proved successful.

Piece of 3/0 steel wool
Small clean can
Dry piece of cloth
Shellac thinner or denatured alcohol
Rubber or plastic gloves (optional)

Steps To Follow:
1. Protect your hands with gloves, if desired.
2. Pour a small amount of denatured alcohol or shellac thinner into a can.
3. Break the pad of steel wool into two equal parts. Immerse one piece of steel wool in the liquid.
4. Rub vigorously over the section containing the white filler. You may use circular motions, but complete the procedure by rubbing with the grain of the wood. Because evaporation occurs quickly, don't do too large an area. You are usually only concerned with tops, so on small commodes, chests, or night stands, you may do the entire top. However, on drop leaf tables, go over each leaf and the top separately.
5. Rub the article with the reserved dry piece of steel wool, and dry it with a cloth.
6. When there is an excessive amount of filler in a depression in the wood, work over this area with your finger tip covered with the wet steel wool.
7. The filler should be gone if you used enough pressure. If not, you should repeat. Now you are ready to proceed with the finishing process.

Removing Refractory Paints
Refractory is a word that means stubborn and is a descriptive term which fits early paints, often homemade, that normal removers will not touch. These were formed from a combination of milk and other ingredients to which some color was added, such as soot from kerosene lamps, earth colors including sienna (brown) or red oxide, or various berry juices. This mixture formed a hard finish. Now modern chemists have a formula for making a casein glue which utilizes milk, so in reality, you are working with a type of glue when you attack this early paint. After removing any finish that is over this paint, try rubbing vigorously with #2 steel wool saturated with water or alcohol. These serve as dissolving agents and can get out a great deal of this paint, but it takes a long time plus diligent effort.

Remember, however, that a purist treasures milk-base paint as an age clue and seeks to preserve it as an historical heritage. Others, who scrub it off, save a small patch on the bottom to indicate how the original finish looked.

Removing Wax

It is not advisable to apply paste wax on bare wood because of the difficulty in removing it if you decide you prefer a different finish. Wax alone is not adequate because accumulations of grime can become intermingled with it, and a dusty, dirty appearance may soon result. If you have a piece that has had such application over the bare wood and you wish to refinish it, proceed as follows. Remove as much wax as you can by immersing a cloth in turpentine and rubbing it vigorously over the surface. Wipe dry with a clean cloth to remove the loosened wax. Probably not all of it will be gone. Therefore, apply a coat of white shellac mixed with an equal amount of shellac thinner or denatured alcohol to prevent the wax from bleeding through. After this dries, you can proceed with any finish you desire—antiquing, painting, or varnishing.

How To Give Pine and Other Light Woods an Old Look

Often it is necessary, because of damage, to add new pieces to vintage pine articles. Whenever possible, old pine should be utilized, but it is not often available and some workers have to resort to new lumber. For example, stripping revealed that a 19th century rope bed which was maple and had attained a fine aged look, had had its two end pieces replaced with new maple. Such recent insertions appear to be stark white and lacking in color or character. If your decision is to do the article naturally, something has to be done to treat the replacement wood in order to make it blend compatibly with the original. Try using a solution of about one pint of ammonia to which you add cut-up bits of one plug of chewing tobacco. Let this combination set for about half an hour before brushing it on the new wood and letting it dry. You may have to do it twice, but the result will be satisfying. You will have attained an aged, mellow tone which, when refinished, will look like a part of the original piece.

Wet Test for Color

A wet test is a means of checking the approximate color the finished piece will be, when done naturally, by wiping a section of it with a rag dampened with turpentine or mineral spirits. This is also the method to follow to see whether there are any imperfections, old finish, or white filler that you thought you had removed left in the grain. Sometimes these are not observable on a dry piece. Their presence indicates that more preparatory work may be necessary. Thus, it's good practice to try a wet test before applying the first coat of finish.

Rubbing Out

After your final finishing coat has dried and you have rubbed your piece with 3/0 steel wool to smooth and cut the gloss, take a clean, flat cloth from which all seams, decorations, buttons, zippers, or other rough places have been removed. Fold it to fit your hand, and rub briskly over the article. This is not a dusting process, so rub hard, with pressure, to produce an even texture. Portions, such as legs, rungs, or slats, can be rubbed with a circular swipe, much as shoes are shined. When this step is done with vigor, a smooth-to-the-touch surface with a soft satin glow will result.

Bar clamps are used to secure the base of this walnut rocker tightly while a cloth clamp holds the top together. Wood should be glued under pressure.

Using Furniture Polishes

In addition to wax, any of the following can serve as a good furniture polish. Commercially produced lemon oil does a fine job and has a pleasant smell. After applying oils to wood, always follow by rubbing them as dry as possible with a clean cloth. Boiled linseed oil has an advantage over other oils, because it produces a harder finish. Mineral oil, the basic ingredient in many polishes, is as good as any, although the odor is not the most pleasing and some additive may be necessary to make it more acceptable (such as a lemon smell to create lemon oil). Try mixing your own polish by adding some odor-yielding agent to mineral oil, like almond, orange, or vanilla. Be careful that alcohol is **not** an ingredient, however, as it could prove harmful to the finish. Fingerprints and grease can be removed just as easily with turpentine. Here, again, the smell turns people to commercial oil polishes.

Making Tack Rags

The most lasting type of homemade tack rag, and one which resembles the commercial kind, can be made as follows. Secure some finely woven cheesecloth, and cut a piece about 1½ to 2 feet square. Dip the cheesecloth in water. Wring it out so it is still wet, but not dripping. Immerse the cloth in a can containing turpentine or mineral spirits, and wring the moisture out. Flatten your damp cheesecloth. Sprinkle it with varnish; then twist the cloth so the varnish is mixed evenly throughout. Fold it into a square (about 4"x4" or 5"x5"). The rag should have a sticky feel. When you wipe dust from a piece of furniture, no moisture should be left on its surface. If any dampness does remain, it means you have not wrung the cloth out well enough. When not in use, keep the tack rag in a tightly closed jar. If it is still clean but beginning to dry out, sprinkle it with some water and turpentine or mineral spirits to revitalize it.

An easy-to-make tack rag that you can use once requires a man's handkerchief or a piece of cloth of about that same size. Immerse it in varnish, wring until all the moisture drops out, and a tacky rag will be the result.

A piece of cloth the approximate size of a handkerchief immersed in turpentine or mineral spirits and wrung until dripless can also function as a tack rag.

Chapter 6

HOW TO COLOR OR
STAIN WOOD

Staining is the method used to darken furniture or other articles constructed of wood. The application of a lighter color will not transform a piece into a lighter shade. For instance, dusky walnut will retain its deep tones and will not resemble golden oak, even when a yellowish hue is brushed on it.

It is not advisable to stain all articles of furniture, for there are certain woods that have innate beauty and are enhanced when left natural. Such woods include cherry, mahogany, and walnut. Pine, maple, and oak may, or may not, be darkened, according to your appreciation of their native, light tones. If you find them attractive as they are, do not apply stain. Check to see how they appear naturally by rubbing a section of the article with a piece of cloth dampened in turpentine. This is called a wet test and dries off rapidly. The color that appears will closely approximate the hue when a clear finish is applied. Then again, if your preference is for darker tones, choose a stain and follow the outlined process. Some other woods which appear to lack character, such as poplar, gumwood, basswood, and certain fruitwoods, are often considered lifeless without color added.

Putting stain directly on a soft wood, such as pine or poplar, is not advisable. Too much will penetrate and the result will be dark and blotchy. Apply a coat of finish first. Either brush on half shellac and half denatured alcohol mixed, or rub on a single coat of varnish with a cloth. Don't apply the varnish with a brush, as this will provide too heavy a covering.

Stores display samples of stain on different kinds of woods. These will give you a truer picture of what result to expect than the examples on chips of paper. For instance, a walnut stain will appear different when applied to pine than it will when rubbed on mahogany, because the intensity of penetration varies according to the type of wood with which you are working. Therefore, be sure you know the tree species so you can check the stained wood samples to see the approximate color you will achieve. The pigments in cans settle to the bottom, so stir thoroughly to acquire an even shade. You will not get the desired tone if any of the coloring matter is left on the bottom of the container.

The four basic stains that are used on furniture are maple (a brownish yellow), mahogany (a reddish brown), walnut (a brown), and oak (a yellow). Trade names for the same tone differ. You can intermix stains to obtain tones of lighter or deeper intensity, according to the effect you wish to produce.

If you prefer, you can make your own stain. It's easy if you mix the proper proportions of the ingredients. Refer to the accompanying charts.

Artist's Oil Pigments	Color
Burnt Umber	Dark brown
Raw Umber	Light brown
Burnt Sienna	Dark red-brown
Raw Sienna	Light yellowish-brown
Van Dyke Brown	Gray-brown
Rose Pink	Red

How To Make Your Own Stains

Jar with a tight lid
Measuring cups
Clean stick for stirring
Boiled linseed oil
Turpentine
Japan Drier
Artist's oil pigment

Color Desired	Oil Pigment
Cherry (dark)	Burnt Sienna
Cherry (light)	2 parts Raw Sienna 3 parts Burnt Sienna
Mahogany (brown)	3 parts Burnt Sienna 1 part Rose Pink 1 part Van Dyke Brown

51

Mahogany (red)	3 parts Burnt Sienna
	2 parts Rose Pink
Oak (dark)	4 parts Raw Sienna
	1 part Burnt Umber
Oak (light)	Raw Sienna
Walnut	4 parts Burnt Umber
	1 part Van Dyke Brown
Maple	Burnt Sienna

Steps To Follow:

1. Combine boiled linseed oil, turpentine, and Japan Drier in a 3-1-½ ratio to produce all the stains mentioned. Add enough artist's oil tube pigment to achieve the desired color. For example, applying this formula, mix 1½ cups boiled linseed oil, ½ cup turpentine, ¼ cup Japan Drier, plus enough selected oil pigment to obtain the color you seek. This makes slightly over a pint of stain.
2. Keep in a tightly covered jar until ready to use.

The ingredients in this homemade stain act as follows: The turpentine carries the mixture into the wood and evaporates. The linseed oil serves as the vehicle to allow an even flow, while the Japan Drier hastens the drying process. The pigment (artist's oils which come in tubes) is the coloring agent. Before opening it, squeeze the tube very gently alternately at one end and then the other four or five times to be sure the pigment is combined with the oil, which tends to rise to the top. Uncap and test some on a piece of paper to see if additional mixing is required.

Before applying the selected stain to the article, remove all of the old finish, and have all surfaces sanded smooth and dust free, because stain will not adhere otherwise.

How To Stain Furniture

Can of stain
Two 2″ brushes
Newspapers
Clean cloths
Latex or rubber gloves
Turpentine or mineral spirits

Steps To Follow:

1. Spread newspapers on the floor beneath the piece.
2. If desired, thin the stain with turpentine so that not as deep a tone is achieved.
3. Apply the stain evenly over the surface with a brush.
4. Allow to stand for about ten minutes, or until the stain flattens in color.
5. You can wipe the stained surface before the recommended time (ten minutes) expires to produce a less intense tone, because this would not permit as much color to penetrate the wood.
6. Using a dry cloth, wipe off the stain remaining on the surface. Proceed in the same sequence that you applied the stain. For example, if you commenced on the left side of the top and then stained a side, wipe the top first from left to right and follow through on the side panel.
7. Use a clean brush to remove any excess stain from crevices and parts the rag won't reach.
8. If the piece appears too dark, some color can be rubbed off with a cloth wet with turpentine while the surface is still wet.
9. Permit the article to dry for about 24 hours, or longer if the humidity is high. If this step is rushed, some of the stain will be picked up when you apply the finish.

Also, never sand until the surface has been sealed (a coat of finish added) because the abrasion will remove some stain and yield a blotched effect. After some experience, and with experimentation, you will learn to control the stain according to your personal preference.

Wearing rubber-type or latex gloves will protect your hands from the absorption of stain in your pores and under your fingernails. These gloves will last indefinitely if they are cared for properly in the following manner. After using the stain, pour some turpentine in a large fruit-type can and, with the gloves still on your hand, immerse them and rub until the color is removed. Dry with a towel. Then wash your gloves with soap and water, while they are still being worn. Wipe excess moisture off them, and hang them up with a clip clothes pin to dry. Now, they will be clean and ready for their next wearing.

When you are staining an article of furniture that has drawers or doors, be sure all of the hardware (hinges, handles, or knobs) are removed. If you just want to do the surface of the door or drawer, you will have to secure newspapers with masking tape over those parts you do not wish to darken. Otherwise the stain will run down the sides and inside. It is perhaps just as easy to do the entire drawer, for you will be giving it some protection against the accumulation of dust. Besides, this is where valuables, clothes, and other items are kept, and you should want this area to be as clean as the rest of the piece.

How To Stain a Small Area on Furniture

Sometimes you will find it necessary to color a small area on an article of furniture. Because of damage, a rather large section of the wood may be missing from an antique, and filler will not suffice to mend it. For example, a portion of the seat of a walnut chair may be absent, an end section of the handkerchief boxes on a cherry chest might be gone, or the panel at the base of a pine church bench could be chipped off. If possible, the missing parts should be replaced with the same type of wood cut to fit tightly and precisely set in place.

If you plan to stain your repaired acquisition, this may enable you to match the color of the inserted part with the original wood in your furniture. However, if natural is your choice, you have to become your own stain mixer. With care and patience, try to achieve a tone to blend in with the mother piece. For such a purpose, it is good to have available a variety of artist's oil colors in tubes and mix them to create the hue you desire. (See chart in next section for guidance.)

How To Stain a Small Area

Varnish
1″ brush
Clean cloths
Artist's oil color (see chart for shade)
Can of stain of the same color as the wood in your piece of furniture
Toothpick or wooden match

Steps To Follow:
1. Varnish the entire article in which you have inserted a repair piece of wood. Proceed with the next step without allowing for drying time, because the color of the wet piece indicates the tone you wish to achieve. Letting it dry will destroy the match in color.
2. Have varnish on a cloth folded to handle easily. Apply it to the replaced section.
3. With a toothpick or wooden match stick, put a dab of oil color on the wet varnish on the repaired surface and stroke with a cloth to blend the color over the entire area.
4. Using the same cloth, follow by dotting some stain from the can and rubbing it gently over the surface with the grain until the proper blend is achieved and the color matches.
5. With your brush, lightly work with the grain over the area so your color blend is even and no dark spots are seen.
6. You may have to repeat steps 3 and 4 if the result is not satisfactory.

54

7. If the surface begins to dry or you are not pleased, the stain may be removed with a damp turpentine rag, and you begin again.
8. Because you are trying to achieve a specific shade, you may need to work in different colors or varying amounts, just like an artist does in trying to create a hue.
9. Allow sufficient drying time (12 hours) before building up with additional coats of finish.

As a specific example of this method, assume that a strip about 6″ long and ½″ wide has been inserted on the front side of a retired pine church bench. Following the application of the varnish, this replacement area remains colorless and white looking, standing out in contrast to the original mellow pine. Select a tube of Van Dyke Brown and a can of maple stain. Add a dab of Van Dyke Brown to this section that is wet with varnish and gently rub with the grain, using the same rag, until an even texture is achieved. Immediately apply a dot of maple stain and stroke this color on until the sought-after tone appears. Brush smooth with a dry brush to blend the toned wood. You should obtain a color similar to, and compatible with, the warm pine patina. The tube pigment tends to darken the wood and remove its bland hue, and the stain gives it a tone to match your piece. The varnish serves as the vehicle which permits the movement of the stains.

The amount of color you rub in determines the depth of the shade you will obtain. The less you use, the softer the hue. The more you apply, the darker the result will be.

You may employ this same method on furniture constructed of different woods in order to blend the entire surface to match. Often a chest of drawers or a commode may be all walnut except for the sides, or a bird's-eye maple chest may have drawer rails or the end panel frames made of lighter maple. Usually the side rungs on walnut cane bottomed chairs are of maple or oak. Other combinations could be listed. The appearance of all these might be improved by the use of this technique.

You may not succeed perfectly in blending the woods to match on the first try and become frustrated, but what artist does not occasionally fail to come up with the desired color on the first try? You might experiment on a scrap of wood in order to get the feel of this special method. Because there's no stain that will produce the exact color you want, you too are stepping into the artist's shoes, and your end result will be successful if you have patience.

Key To Blending Stains To Match Woods

On articles made of:	Artist's Oil Tube Color and Stain
Cherry	Burnt Sienna Cherry Stain
Mahogany	Burnt Sienna Mahogany Stain
Maple	Van Dyke Brown Maple Stain
Oak	Raw Sienna Maple Stain
Pine	Van Dyke Brown Maple Stain
Walnut	Burnt Umber Walnut Stain

Chapter 7

HOW TO ANTIQUE
FURNITURE

Antiquing, as the term is employed today, is the method of applying a color (white, green, blue, or your choice) over a piece of furniture, as is or stripped down, rubbing in brown tones to obtain a streaked effect, and touching up the high decorative details with gold. For those of you who prefer color rather than natural or stained wood, this technique is helpful.

There are sometimes excuses for such a treatment of an old piece. For instance, a petite, one drawer, one door stand was constructed of five different woods, as though the cabinetmaker threw in all the scraps in his shop to fashion it. Its owner dubbed it the "Ugly Duckling," but through antiquing this quaint misfit emerged as a fairy tale swan.

Or, a mother might consider a black walnut Victorian bedroom set too dark for her little girl's room and could choose to antique it in light shades, knowing that the paint can always be removed if she desires to restore it to its natural state again.

Antiquing also helps to unite uncoordinated pieces of furniture into a set or suite and can help achieve an attractive room appearance on an exhausted budget. For example, scrounging in secondhand stores might yield a dressing table with decorative wood trim garlands, a chest with ornate brass hardware, and a plain bed. If the lines of these unmatched pieces are compatible, they may become a unit by antiquing them to match. If you employ white paint with dark umber tones and highlights of gold, a feminine French Provincial-type ensemble will be the result.

Some pieces of early 20th century furniture lend themselves to this technique. Rockers, built to resemble the Boston type, were often painted black. Commonly a red aniline dye was applied to maple to give furniture a feigned cherry or mahogany appearance. These finishes are most difficult to remove, since remnants of black or red tend to remain in the fibers and pores of the wood. Antiquing disguises them and can result in gay, charming focal points for your home, especially when an accent color is picked up from a room's upholstery, draperies, or carpeting.

How to Antique Furniture: Method I

Mineral spirits or turpentine
Two 2″ brushes, one for paint, one for shellac
Varnish
White shellac, 3 or 4 lb. cut
Shellac thinner or denatured alcohol
A tube of burnt umber (or any artist oil color tube, depending on the tone effect you desire)
Clean cloths
Several small clean cans to hold the color mixtures
A small can of flat or semi-gloss paint, the color of your choice, either oil or water base
Tube or powdered gold (called bronzed colors), obtainable at a paint store
Bronzing lacquer (optional)
Lacquer thinner, if bronzing lacquer is used.

Steps To Follow:

1. For best results, start with the bare wood. It is not the most lasting method to cover an old painted, varnished, or stained surface. It may not adhere well or could chip. (See Chapter 3 for paint removing and sanding instructions.) However, if you plan to cover the existing finish, remove any wax from the piece by giving it a turpentine bath (see directions in Chapter 5). Sand any rough spots and fill any cracks or holes with wood putty to be sure that the surface is clean and smooth.

2. Apply the paint with a 2″ brush, starting at the top and working down, to prevent drips on the already painted areas. Allow to dry thoroughly. The length of time will depend on whether you have a water base or an oil base paint. Water base sometimes dries as rapidly as thirty minutes, depending on the humidity, but it is best to wait several hours before you begin the next step. Oil base, on the other hand, will need to stand overnight or approximately 12 hours.

3. When the surface is thoroughly dry, check to see whether the paint has adequately covered all areas. If it has, you may proceed with the next step. Otherwise, you should apply a second coat.

4. Clean your brush after each use. For water base, rinse the excess paint off with water, and then wash with soap and water, rinse again, and set aside to dry. A brush with oil base paint on it should be immersed in a clean can containing turpentine, followed by a soap and water bath. Rinse and permit it to dry.

5. Stir the white shellac, 3 or 4 lb. cut. Make a combination of half shellac and half shellac thinner or denatured alcohol. Brush on with even strokes, being careful that this thin mixture does not run down on the unfinished sections and become gummy before you can stroke it out. Shellac is affected by both age and humidity. Never use any that is over six months old. Since high humidity will influence the drying time and the ultimate finish, choose a day to apply it when there is not too much dampness in the air. Also, nylon brushes are recommended for shellac, because with bristle brushes small pieces are apt to be deposited on the surface and only show up after the article dries.

6. When this shellac coating is dry (in about 3 or 4 hours), rub the item briskly with 3/0 steel wool to cut the gloss. Vacuum well and dust with a tack rag.

7. You are now ready to apply the glaze and begin antiquing. Mix about ½ teaspoon of burnt umber (or any other dark oil color) with ¼ cup of varnish. This amount will do one chair; if your object is larger, double the amounts. Brush this on your article, doing small sections at a time. Then wipe each portion with a clean cloth, so the dark shade is mostly removed from the high spots and fades out toward the center of panels, tops, rungs, etc. to simulate a worn look. Wipe in streaking motions to develop the lines. The tone of the streaked effect will be dependent on the oil color you select. (See chart in Chapter 6 for tones of oil colors.)

8. If this glazing mixture begins to seem too sticky, dampen a cloth with turpentine and proceed as before. Allow to dry before starting step 9. Twelve hours should be sufficient depending, of course, on the humidity. High humidity slows down the drying time of any finishing material and should always be taken into consideration before you start a project.

9. Mix about 6 teaspoons of varnish with about 4" of gold as it comes out of the tube, or so that it has a thick enough consistency to cover and color the surface. Too much varnish will make it thin and runny. You may have to adjust the formula to satisfy your needs. If you are using powdered gold, add about a level teaspoon to 3 teaspoons of varnish. Mix either combination well. Bronzing lacquer, which is obtainable where artists' oil colors are sold, may be substituted for varnish in about the same proportions. It comes in small 2½ ounce bottles and is advantageous because it dries faster than varnish. Dip a cloth into

this mixture and rub over the raised and decorated parts. Wipe any excess off with a dry cloth. The effect you wish to obtain will be determined by the amount you leave on the surface.

10. If you get too much gold on, a rag immersed in turpentine will remove it. However, if you have used bronzing lacquer, you will have to dampen your cloth with lacquer thinner instead.

11. Let the surface dry for 24 hours before rubbing the piece lightly with 3/0 steel wool. Vacuum to remove steel wool particles, and then clean any excess with a tack rag. Wax or oil the surface, and it is ready to be placed in your home.

How to Antique Furniture: Method 2

A commercial antiquing kit purchased at a paint, hardware, or department store.

Steps To Follow:

Obey the manufacturer's directions as stated in the kit.

Regardless of the condition of the furniture you have, the "antique it" method can be used to produce effective results. Probably you have seen samples of such furniture in paint stores as a promotional way to sell kits. Because manufacturers have done considerable research in developing their merchandise, they are well qualified to tell you how to use their products, so obey their instructions in order to achieve the best results.

Chapter 8

MIGHTY OAK PROVOKES RENEWED INTEREST

Oak, widely known for its strength (and heft), is an open-grained wood ideal for furniture making which has finally come into its own as the "in" type with the young collectors of today. These sometimes massive, and always durable, pieces are the "antiques" they remember from their childhood, just as walnut and mahogany were the heritage woods associated with the youthful days of their parents.

An oak schoolmaster's desk, painted green when found, has been refinished naturally to show its pronounced grain.

61

Oak pieces are being sought and bought widely as an investment for the future. Actually, this species may be the last vestige of the well-constructed, long-lasting furniture of the pre-plastic antique age. Realizing that oak would some day reign as queen again, collectors and dealers have been hoarding these pieces, and now the rush is on. That it is still readily obtainable is apparent when one visits antique shops or estate and garage sales, but when one examines the price tags, there is nothing inexpensive on those labels. Imagine how your money could have grown if you had had the foresight, say five years ago, to purchase ten round, oak, dining room tables, ten secretary desks, and the same number of hall trees that once held hats and coats on their ornamental hooks. An investment then of $750 would have ascended to roughly $6,000 on today's market. However, don't despair, for there are many articles constructed from this wood still selling at moderate prices if you have the time to search, and you too may share the profits anticipated in the future.

When you find an oak piece, you have to decide what approach you are going to use to domesticate it. Any of the techniques outlined earlier in the book—use it as it is, revitalize it with an oil cleansing, or revive it with a water, oil and turpentine bath—may satisfy your needs and save you time. If you wish to rejuvenate it to the utmost and accentuate its grain and features, a complete refinishing job is the route to take.

This oak tavern table knew much hard service, as shown by all the signs of wear on its edges.

Refinishing oak pieces can be fun and offers no real problems. The key is a thorough paint removing in order to strip the old finish completely and clean the pores adequately. Because of its coarse grain, more stain, filler, or paint is apt to be left in the pores than with other types of wood, unless certain measures are taken to prevent it.

As a suggested method, work on small sections of an article at a time in order to achieve greater efficiency. Disassemble tables, chairs, or other items that will easily separate, and remove all hardware. When each section has been stripped, sanded, and is ready for the finishing stage, reassemble the piece. The hardware should be cleaned while it is off and returned to its original position only after the resuscitating process is completed.

The straight lines of a child's rocker represent Mission Oak, circa 1895-1900, which has experienced a recent revival in popularity.

Probably the water-wash method of paint removing, as outlined in Chapter 3, will produce the most satisfactory results. This is recommended because the water will penetrate the open grain and wash away most of the filler, stain, or paint. The other stripping method tends to leave the pores clogged, because, as you scrape the surface off, you do little to attack and draw out the residue which has penetrated.

However, add an additional step. After the piece has been stripped and cleaned off with steel wool and water, wipe the excess moisture off with a dry towel. Then, apply another coat of remover over the damp surface, and allow the remover to remain on the surface for approximately 10 minutes (more won't hurt). Then with #2 steel wool and water, rub vigorously with the grain. Rinse thoroughly with clean water, and dry with an absorbent cloth.

Thorough washing with clean water is essential. Otherwise a gray cast may appear on the piece when it is dry, and it will assume a faded-out appearance. This is caused by a residue left by water and some softened agents in the stain, filler, or paint that have not been adequately washed away. It, however, will not be evident if the piece is antiqued or stained. If a natural finish is applied, a cloudy effect may be discovered.

You can attack this dullness in one of two ways. You might paint-remove the piece again, but this results in a time-consuming chore. Instead, you may wash the piece with full strength household bleach, placed in a can, and applied with a rag. Let it dry, and you will notice a cleaner aspect.

Varnish is an excellent finish. If you are not adept with a brush, the rag application method is recommended. In addition to its fast drying time, it is almost run-proof. Because it doesn't stay wet long, very little foreign matter will adhere to the surface. This, in itself, is valuable to you, for it will eliminate sanding between coats.

An electric sander is an aid when working with oak—on table tops, chests, and commodes which have large flat surfaces and on other articles that have uninterrupted planes. The hardness of the wood makes this method an asset and will save much wear and fatigue on arms, which tend to become sandpaper weary. Areas with carving or designs must, of course, be hand sanded, but you will find that the result is worth your while when you show the finished piece to an exclaiming, complimenting friend.

Join the oak rush, if you will, but don't rush the job.

A former store piece, an oak double spool cabinet now functions as a table, making an interesting conversation piece in a home.

Chapter 9

HOW TO CURE A
BOTTOMLESS SEAT

Cane is split rattan (from a climbing palm with a long, slender stem) used to weave chair seats. Besides the natural product from the tree, plastic cane has been developed, and many craftsmen find it dependable. However, it seems more compatible with an antique to combine it with the authentic rattan.

There are two general forms: hand caning, a weaving process; and pressed caning, available in pre-woven sheets. If hand caning is required, there will be holes drilled approximately equidistant in the wood around the seat of the chair. Sometimes a back requires this treatment also.

Pressed caning can be recognized because there is a narrow groove incised in the wood around the seat or the back of the chair. Both these processes will be described. It is important to note that, like most cloth, natural cane has a right and a wrong side. The shiny, smooth front should be on top; the rough, dull back should be on the underneath.

Usually, cane is purchased by the hank, and, depending on their size, three or four seats can be woven from one hank. Many dealers will not sell less than this amount. Some retailers may let you purchase one strand of binding, which should be enough to complete several chairs. Since so little is required, it is difficult to use up a whole hank of binder. Some companies sell kits with enough material to complete one seat, but this can be an expensive way to buy if you have a set to do. Cane which is saved for years may become dried out and should be discarded as it snaps and breaks easily. Only that with some spring in it should be utilized.

If the old cane is in the chair, it must be cut out and the holes cleared of any ends, remover, or anything else that would clog them and prevent the new cane from entering. This process can be accomplished with a small knife blade, a pointed instrument such as an awl, a nail punch, or a pick, or it can be drilled out.

It is less complicated to learn on a square seat because some deviation in pattern is necessary on chair bottoms with other shapes.

How To Determine the Size of Cane Needed

With a ruler measure the distance between the holes drilled in the wood and their diameter to determine which width of cane is required.

Cane Size	Diameter	Distance between holes
superfine (narrowest)	1/8	3/8
fine fine	3/16	1/2
fine	3/16	5/8
medium	1/4	3/4
common (widest)	5/16	7/8

How To Cane a Chair by Hand

Remember, your chair should be completely repaired, reglued, and the finish should be as you desire it before you cane it.

Cane the desired size, see chart above
Strand of binding
8 or 10 clip-type clothes pins, or a like number of rubber bands
Pan or a pail of water
Two towels
Some small instrument, such as a nail file, awl, nut pick, or etc.
Scissors
6 or 8 pegs with which to hold the cane in place. A dowel stick tapered at the end to fit the hole is recommended. Sometimes golf tees or fat pencils will suffice.
On a square seat, 4 wooden pegs sized to fit in the corner holes are needed.
Hammer is required for the final step, to pound pegs in the corners of a square seat to hold the binder in place. A nail punch is helpful also.

Steps To Follow:

1. Pulling out one strand from the hank at a time, remove as much cane as you feel you will work with at one sitting. Roll each into a circle (such as you might wrap a cord or a skein of yarn). Clip individually with a clothespin, or slip a rubber band loosely around each one, or devise your own method to prevent tangling.

2. Fill the pan or pail with warm water and place the circles in it. Cover with a towel. Soak about half an hour before using. Remove only one piece of cane at a time, and keep the others immersed. If

Before. A refinished walnut chair, shown before it is caned.

preferred, the remainder can be kept moist by wrapping them in the damp towel. Water makes the cane more pliable. When it dries it tends to tighten.

3. Use the dry towel to keep the wood wiped off so the finish will not be damaged by contact with the soaked cane.

4. The nail file, nut pick, awl, or other instrument is used to probe gently up and down to keep the holes in the chair open or to lift a strand pressed against the bottom so that loose ends can be looped under and tied off.

5. The scissors are for cutting as needed. Weave back and forth with a continuous strand as many times as possible.

6. Cane should always be pliable. Unwind one pre-soaked strand. With the glossy side uppermost, run it through your fingers. Is the cane broken anywhere? Are the eyes (joints where the stem grew out) bent and rough? There will be some roughness, but the smoother end of the joint should be drawn through the weaving steps first to minimize the friction and reduce wear. Are there any slits or slivers? Inspect each piece of cane prior to using it, and cut away any damaged sections. Now you are ready to begin the 7 step weaving process. Some people like to work standing up with the chair on a table. Others prefer to sit on the floor or bend over from another chair. Assume the posture which is easiest for you, but keep the front of the seat near you as you face the chair.

After. A refinished walnut chair, complete with a hand-caned seat.

Important: CONSULT THE DIAGRAMS AS YOU WORK.

1. Count the holes in the wood at the back of the seat. Place a peg in the middle hole. If there are an even number of holes, there will be two middle ones and both should be pegged. Now count the holes in the front of the chair and treat it in a similar manner.
2. Work from the center to one side of the frame. Take the inspected damp strand of cane, glossy side uppermost, and remove a middle peg at the rear. Insert the end of the strand in the hole from the top of the chair to the bottom. Loop the cane up around the inside frame and insert it in the same hole again. This loose end, about 2"-3" long, should be tied underneath (see diagram 1) when there is a strand to secure it to. Let the long section of the cane cover the looped portion.

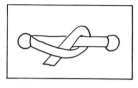

Diagram 1

Push in a peg to hold the end tightly. Pull the strand vertically across to the front of the seat, remove the peg there, and put the cane in the hole from the top, straight across from the back insertion. Pull taut. Replace the peg to hold the cane securely. Underneath, cross to the adjoining hole in the front, bring the cane up from the bottom to the top, and pull across to insert in the corresponding hole at the rear. Pull the strand all the way through until it is tight. Remove the front peg and replace it in the back hole you have just entered. You now have two parallel lines front to back across the chair. Let the peg follow the strand into each hole as you work to keep the cane tight. Slip the strand through your fingers each time to be sure it is not twisted and the shiny side is always up. Continue the process to cover half the seat with straight lines. Do not enter the corner hole on a square chair. Use a new strand if necessary but merely insert the cane in the hole and push a peg in to hold it. Do not loop it around the frame as was done at the middle. Peg any loose ends. Always leave 2 or 3 inches of cane at the start and finish for tying off purposes. Tilt the chair upside down and tie as you go when possible. See step 1.

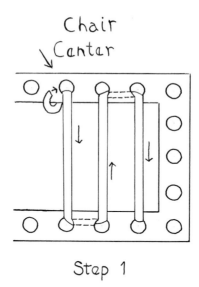

Step 1

3. Repeat the same process working from the center to the other side of the seat.
4. Starting at the front or the back of the chair, lay lines horizontally across the top of the cane which is already in position. Push a peg

70

in the hole to hold each beginning and ending piece of cane in place. Use another peg to follow your strand into each hole in turn to keep it taut. See Step 2.

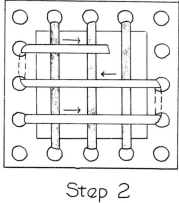

Step 2

5. Beginning at either edge of the chair, following the same procedure and entering the same holes as used in the first step, lay parallel lines of cane from front to back vertically across the chair, placing them to the right. Employ pegs as before. See Step 3.

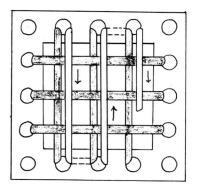

Step 3

6. Now you are ready to begin your first real weaving step. One hand should be underneath and the other on top of the existing cane, except when one hand is needed to prevent the strand from twisting while the other is pulling through. The strands which were placed in position last are to be lashed to the right of the original lines. Start at the front left. The cane will be inserted into the same holes and will parallel the horizontal lines which were established in the second step.

71

Always go on the same side of the existing horizontals, permitting an established strand to be nearest the front of the chair and weaving above it. Go under the original vertical and over the last vertical, binding it to the right, under the original vertical, over the last laid vertical, under, over, under, over across the seat. Do only as much as you can pull through easily without breaking the cane. If a piece splits or breaks, take a new strand. Employ a continuous strand when possible, not one cut to size. Continue placing pegs as per previous instructions until there are two horizontal lines in each hole. When returning from the right, the rhythm is reversed to over, under, over, under. See Step 4.

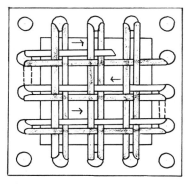

Step 4

7. Turn the chair bottom side up. Tie the loose ends by inserting them under the existing loops. An instrument, such as a nail file, awl, nut pick, or the like, will help to lift the loop gently to slip the end under it. Trim the secured ends to about ½″ in length. Remove pegs after completing this process. Ends which have dried out can be dampened with a wet cloth for ease in working. Square off lines with your fingers.
8. Now you are ready for the first diagonal. Start at the left corner hole in front. Go under the two vertical lines, over the two horizontal lines, under the vertical, over the horizontal, until you have slanted across the entire seat. Use pegs as before. Continue until each diagonal is completed. Do not try to pull too large a section through at one time. The cane forms a straight line and is not too difficult to pull if you are doing this step correctly. Tie ends. See Step 5.

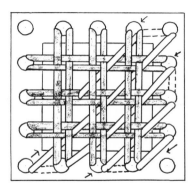

Step 5

9. Beginning at the right front corner hole, proceed in the same manner diagonally across the chair in the opposite direction, only this time go over the vertical, under the horizontal, over the vertical, under the horizontal until the entire seat is crossed. Be sure all ends are tied when finished. See Step 6.

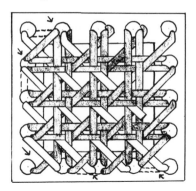

Step 6

10. The binding is a thicker, wider cane and covers the holes to give the seat a finished appearance. It is laid on top of the holes in the frame and a piece of regular cane (possibly with the tip cut to a point for ease in inserting) is used to secure it in place. Pre-soak each for greater pliability. On a square seat, cut 4 pieces of binding to fit each side, allowing enough extra to go down from top to bottom through the corner holes. Lay the binder over the holes in the frame. Start at the first hole from a corner. Coming from the bottom, bring the regular strand of cane up on one side of the binder, cross over it, and

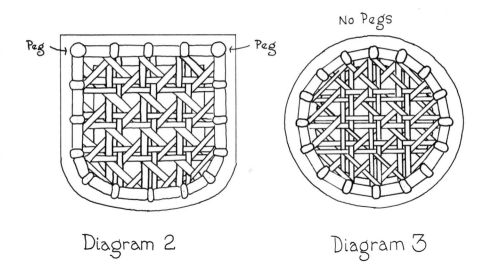

Diagram 2   Diagram 3

push the end down in the same hole. Pass underneath the seat to the adjoining hole and come up, over the binding and down. Continue until this piece is secured. Repeat all around the seat. The fastening process may be done in every hole unless they are close together or clogged with cane, in which case every other one may be used. (Let your small instrument—file, awl, pick—gently push the clogging cane aside in the hole.) Place the loose ends of the binders in the corner holes and with the hammer pound a peg in place flush with the frame to hold the ends. A nail punch helps with this process. The peg always remains in the seat. On a round seat, corner pegs are not required. Instead, the binder is overlapped at the back of the seat for 2 or 3 holes and secured by the cane. A semi-round frame might require pegs at the 2 rear corners. See Step 7 and Diagrams 2 and 3.

Round or half-round seats may demand slight deviations and the pattern may vary a little at the edges, but try to make it as perfect as possible. Sometimes the cane must go down, in, and up through the same hole on a diagonal. This is referred to as dovetailing. It is necessary to skip a row temporarily and come back later or to take a new piece of cane in order to do this.

Cane should be tightly woven so that the new seat does not sag but remains taut and firm. Some people darken the cane with stain and shellac it. Since drying out causes damage, it seems preferable to leave it natural and to go over it occasionally with a water dampened cloth on both the top and bottom sides.

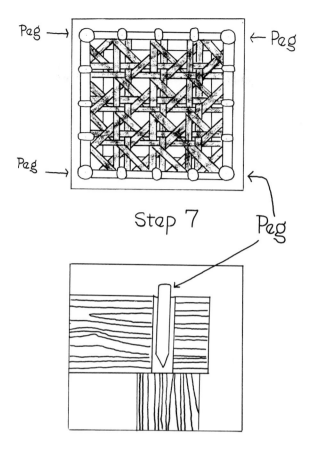

Peg → ← Peg

Peg →

Step 7

Peg

Some chair backs do not have holes drilled in the outer frame but have them in inserts nailed on the four sides. It may be wise, in order to keep them from pulling out, to glue and screw these pieces being careful not to block a hole. Drilling a hole first and waxing the point helps the screw go in easily. It is necessary to leave the cane loose in the first few steps to accommodate back curvature. The degree of slack will depend on the shape. The diagonal steps will draw the pattern tight.

Don'ts include: Never step on a strand as you work since cane breaks and splits. Do not permit children to pick at the seat. Never stand on a cane chair. Don't place a cushion on a cane seat, as this puts pressure on certain spots and can cause undue wear.

Usually the cost of professional hand caning is determined by the number of holes in the wooden frame. Count them and multiply by the price per hole to find the cost.

How To Insert a Pressed Cane Seat

Note: Your chair should be glued, repaired, and finished as desired before the caning is attempted.

Sheet of pressed cane of the required size
Spleen to hold it in the grooves
Hide or white glue
Hammer
Board as long as the seat and about ½″ wide
Chisel to pry out the old spleen
Pail or pan
Towel
Scissors
Cloths

Before. An unfinished maple-oak pressed-cane kitchen chair, showing the spleen that secures the cane in the incised groove.

Steps To Follow:
1. Pressed cane is purchased by the inch or foot in pre-woven sheets.
2. Cut out the old cane. The spleen in the groove is glued in place and softened with water and pried up with sharp cutting chisels. Be careful, as it is easy to get badly cut while doing this.
3. Measure the seat bottom and cut the cane sheet to allow ample extra for inserting in the groove all around the seat. Any excess can be trimmed off at the end. Measure enough spleen to fit the groove.
4. Put warm water in a pail or pan. Soak the cane and spleen for half an hour until pliable.
5. Put a generous amount of glue in the groove, enough so it will seep out when the spleen is added. Fit the sheet of cane over the seat, and, with your fingers, push the edges of the cane into the groove. Place the spleen, cut to exact size, into position over the cane in the

After. A refinished and reglued maple-oak kitchen chair, complete with its new pressed-cane seat.

groove. Position the edge of the board on top of the spleen and hammer it down into the groove all the way around the frame. Dampen a cloth with water to wipe off the excess glue which oozes up. Wipe dry.

6. The sheet of cane should be pulled taut and should not sag. It will tighten slightly when it dries.

Usually the cost is reckoned by the number of inches of cane required to do the job, at so much per inch, if done professionally.

Chapter 10

HOW ABOUT ACCESSORY
OBJECTS?

Copper, Brass, and Bronze

You just couldn't pass up that blackened copper wash boiler with the low, low price which you saw at that recent yard sale, but, now that you have it, what are you going to do with it? It would look great polished bright with pots of gay scarlet geraniums in it or as a wood box placed by the fireplace to catch the lights from the flickering flames on the hearth. It could even be a magazine rack beside Gramp's favorite recliner, or, since a boiler is a collectible rather than a bonafide antique, it could be sliced in half to be used as wall planters. Yes, it was too good a buy to pass up, but now what?

Your first try could be paint remover. Apply thoroughly over the boiler and rub vigorously with 3/0 steel wool. Some of the crusted grime may be removed in this manner. If much still remains, use scouring powder and 3/0 steel wool saturated in water, rubbing in the same direction over the entire piece. Several applications are often necessary, and hard rubbing is essential. If this removes most of the heavy concentration, then you can employ a commercial brass or copper cleaner to bring out the luster. Always follow the maker's directions.

But if lacquer has been applied to brass, bronze, or copper items, cleansing agents cannot work properly. It is first necessary to strip off the coating with paint remover in order to permit the cleaner to function. Vinegar, with its acetic acid content, provides a home remedy for counteracting tarnish on objects such as wash boilers or other heavily coated items. Instructions for its application follow.

79

How To Clean Brass, Bronze and Copper with Vinegar

White vinegar
Newspapers, paper toweling, or rags
#3/0 steel wool
Two buckets
Detergent
Clean cloths

Steps To Follow:
1. Large items, such as wash boilers, may be coated with newspapers, paper toweling, or rags soaked in vinegar and wrapped around their surfaces. Small articles may be put in a bucket containing vinegar.
2. Permit the small objects to remain in this liquid for a few minutes. Then, check to see if the tarnish is being loosened by rubbing briskly with 3/0 steel wool. If so, remove the article and rub thoroughly with steel wool until all of the tarnish has disappeared. Wash with a detergent and warm water, rinse, and dry.
3. Be careful not to leave these small objects in the vinegar solution too long, because a copper toned film can develop on brass.
4. Large articles that are deeply tarnished should be left for about ten minutes with the wet vinegar wrapping. After this time, you can check the action of the vinegar by rubbing briskly with 3/0 steel wool. If the coating seems to be sufficiently loosened, rub the entire surface with 3/0 steel wool moistened in vinegar. If, however, the vinegar action is not complete, wet the covering with more of it, and permit it to stand until you check it again.
5. After most of the tarnish has been removed by the steel wool-vinegar procedure, use a commercial copper or brass cleaner to complete the job.
6. Mix warm water and a detergent and wash the pieces thoroughly, rinse, and dry.
7. Buff lightly with a dry piece of 3/0 steel wool, and polish with a soft cloth. You may use a metal polish to bring out the glow of the metal.

A touch of the hands is all that is necessary to leave darkened spots on unprotected brass or copper. Therefore, it is good to wear gloves or to use a cloth when it is necessary to move objects fashioned from these metals. Otherwise, personal contact should be avoided. Some people like to put lacquer from a spray can over the surface to ward off tarnish. Lacquer dries so rapidly that it is difficult to use. It must be sprayed quickly and evenly or the result will be blotchy. If you choose to use this product, be careful not to inhale the strong vapors.

There are people who prefer to permit their metals to acquire patina and do not want them polished. Such a woman was out driving in a Swede-filled community in Illinois one hot summer day. She was going up a steep hill when she spied a man pouring water from a shiny teakettle into his automobile radiator. Oblivious to the danger of creating a traffic problem, she strained to look at the kettle and was positive it was an antique piece she'd like to acquire, but, when she stopped to contact the owner, she found he treasured it. Afterwards, as she related her tale to sympathetic ears, her concluding comment conveyed disapproval, "You could tell that man was a Swede because only a Swede would polish copper to a gleam like that!"

But, sometimes, even a person of Scandinavian origin should be wary before cleaning a time-was object. The greenish coating which copper (a metal in itself), brass (an alloy of copper and zinc), or bronze (a combination of copper and tin) may develop is referred to as "verdigris." At times, companies attempt to imitate this cast on their new products. Once an antiquer acquired a brass desk set with greenish overtones, and, finding this unattractive, commenced the cleaning process. A knowledgeable friend happened in and was horrified! Marked "Tiffany," this set was a product of the famous New York shop and the verdigris was an applied artistic finish of theirs. Strip it off? No way! This must be retained, or some of the value would wash down the drain.

In addition, there are authorities who specialize in ancient brass, bronze, and copper who chant, "Do not remove the green patina of antique metals, or spoil their coloring with cleaning." These purists are concerned with the genuinely antique articles, not with a "modern" (to them) fifty-year-old wash boiler which they would dub a "young un". These connoisseurs would permit a housewife to take her fresh lemon or grapefruit rind, turn it inside out, dip it in salt, and use it to rub over the metals to remove stains. She could then wash and polish the metals with a soft cloth. This method does not destroy patina and just think how economical it is to eat a grapefruit or bake a lemon pie, then use the empty "shells" as a cleaner.

So, if you like gleam, be a Swede and polish; but if you don't, or if you find you have an "induced Tiffany Tarnish," or if you have a genuine antique, let your metal retain its haze.

Rejuvenating Iron

Rust results from the union of oxygen in the air with iron in a process called oxidation, and moisture is a large contributing factor to this change. The surface of the metal is eaten away or corroded. If the rust has not been forming for too long, it will help to scrub the surface with water and a wire-bristled brush, and then use naval jelly or other rust removers, which are available commercially. Follow the directions on the container for proper procedures. Abrasive action, through rubbing with sandpaper or #2 steel wool, will often help remove some of the roughness on more stubborn pieces.

Most antiquers warn that you spray away value when you use flat black paint on old items and would scorn this approach. It is possible to rub on old-fashioned stove polish, the kind your grandparents used. This can serve an important role in revitalizing antiques that have iron appendages, such as the bases of ice cream tables and chairs or the cutting edges of old tools. Once the finish has been removed, if there is any, and the rust has been cleaned off, and the item is free of dirt, apply a coat of stove polish with a rag or brush. Let it stand for a time; then rub briskly until a warm gun-metal glow appears. This finish resembles the original given to metals such as these and is more natural looking than painting with a flat black. The stove polish coating should be protected with an application of varnish or by spraying with an aerosol can of clear finish. If this is not done, the black will eventually rub off.

Care of Marble

Many people think that marble, because it is stone, is sturdy and strong, when, in reality, it demands tender care. It is limestone in a more or less crystalline state, stains easily, and is affected by acid. The following are some points to remember.

Marble reacts readily to heat and cold and can crack if it is exposed to a rapid temperature change. For example, if a slab is taken out of a heated house when the winter temperature is around freezing, it should be wrapped in a blanket to avoid damage.

Whenever is is moved, marble should be insulated against jarring and bumping by wrapping it in a blanket and laying it flat. This will help to prevent chipping and cracking.

This stone is porous, so moist glasses set on its surface can cause rings. Always wipe off spills immediately to prevent stains.

It is possible to wash marble with detergent and warm water, rinse with clear water, and buff by rubbing it briskly with a woolly cloth. If it does not polish well, a gloss may be achieved by covering the surface with a paste wax, following the manufacturer's directions on the can.

Originally, marble was not applied over a wooden top but merely had a frame to support it. Thus, a "double top" would make a buyer suspect that the marble was acquired later. Also, the stone was usually cut to be compatible with the lines of the piece it enhanced, with rounded edges if the wood was rounded off, square corners if the frame was squared, or similar considerations as to style. Take notice of these details before you buy, because the article would not be authentic if the marble is offered as an added attraction rather than as a part of the original design.

Chapter 11

BEAT-UP FRAMES
RECEIVE ALLURE

It is often possible to acquire beat-up picture frames at charity resale shops, garage sales, auctions, antique stores, or from attics. These can be converted into dramatic additions to wall groupings.

When a creative woman wanted to display family tree pictures in miscellaneous and assorted frames (some lacy, some plain, some gold, some stained) above an antique day bed in her family room, she cut out a pattern of each framed daguerreotype and photograph. With gummed tape stuck on the back of each outline, she made the patterns adhere to the wall and arranged and rearranged the ovals and rectangles until the overall result was pleasing in balance and form. In order to be sure, she left them for a few days so she could recheck her display. When she was contented that she liked what she saw, she was ready to pound in picture nails to hold this miscellaneous family grouping. The proprietor of a gift shop recommends a similar solution. She advocates laying the various objects on the floor to seek their best relationship before they are hammered into place.

There are a variety of ways to renovate discarded frames. An interior designer wanted that feminine touch above the bed in his little daughter's room. He secured an oversized print of an old fashioned girl in her full, floor-sweeping gown and antiqued an old, deep frame with golds and the exact shade of blue in the depicted dress to compliment the picture. This was indeed a dainty solution to the transformation of a cast-off. (See Chapter VII on antiquing techniques.)

An artist needed a rustic effect to enhance a still life pencil sketch of a weathered wagon wheel, coal scuttle, pumpkin, scoop, and dipper. His choice was a worn dark frame. Using 120 grit, he sandpapered over the old finish, rubbing harder at some spots and less heavily at others, to yield a blotched appearance of dark and light contrasts. Next, with a brush, he delicately stroked on some white paint and wiped most of it off with a cloth, leaving only the merest slivers of white in the ridges. His rural sketch seemed perfectly coordinated in its intentionally battered-appearing frame.

There are additional ways to achieve that personality-plus status.

Sometimes a plain pine frame was built up with layers of plaster of Paris and gilted to give it a glamorous aspect. This often becomes tattered in appearance. Several remedies are possible. Take off the color with paint remover. Then, place the frame in a tub of warm water to soften the plaster of Paris. Cover it with a towel to keep it damp all over, and permit it to remain until the outer surface seems to be soaking off. This treatment will remove the coating, perhaps with an assist from the prying strokes of a putty knife or chisel. Wipe off the moisture thoroughly with an absorbent cloth, and put aside until the wood is entirely dry (about 24 hours) before sanding and applying finish. (See Chapter 3.) Pine frames are not available in quantities, so a natural approach is desirable when that wood is exposed. However, if stain seems indispensible, consult Chapter 6 for directions.

When plaster of Paris frames retain most of their original surface, but some sections or pieces have broken off, there are two ways to restore these damaged parts. First, by using plaster of Paris mixed according to the manufacturer's directions, you can build up the surface by matching it to a similar design on the frame. You can readily shape the plaster while wet and then give it a finished touch with a small file, knife, or sandpaper when it has dried. Add gold as directed in the next step. Secondly, you may proceed by applying a coat of oil over a matching section that is perfect. Then apply wet plaster of Paris over the section, pressing firmly so that, when it dries, you have a mold. Grease the inside of it and pack it with wet plaster of Paris. After the mixture dries, remove the molded piece, sand, file, cut off any excess, and glue it into place. Regilt as directed below.

Where slight flecks of gold are missing from a gilt frame, it is possible to apply a little patching color from a commercial tube of "gold leaf." Squeeze out a small amount and put it on with a finger tip or a cloth. If you prefer, you may use a metal leaf bronzing powder as directed in Chapter 7.

There are resuscitation tactics possible with shoe polish. After stripping, this colored wax can be rubbed into a frame. Always use the paste variety. Brown shades could cover a dark wood, such as walnut, while a neutral is compatible with light-colored species, such as pine or maple. Rub on a coat of polish with a rag, working in small circles and finishing by smoothing out with the grain of the wood. Shine with a cloth between coats. Apply a second layer also with the grain, and continue until the desired build up is achieved. Then wipe off any excess with a clean cloth, and the frame is ready for hanging.

It is almost unbelievable what appears these days as wall decorations. Grandma's thin wire-rimmed spectacles and her gold watch that doesn't tick any more; Dad's lead soldiers, which he molded when he was a lad; medals; wild flower mementoes from a vacation; documents such as indentured servant agreements; invitations or homestead deeds; paper dolls; illustrations from old magazines and books; hand-painted plates; buttons, campaign badges, or pins; parts of old watches, such as wheels or cases; keys—the list seems to never end. Often it is necessary to attach the objects to a background with glue or by sewing them into place. For primitive articles, such as toy soldiers, a burlap background might be sought. Velvet, which picks up the color of a minor flower on china or a tone in a garment on a portrait plate, elegantly accentuates this hue when it is incorporated into the backdrop. Drawers in which printers used to keep their type or ecology boxes form antique showcases also.

At many libraries it is possible to borrow pictures which can be put on display in your home until you decide which ones you prefer. Some frame shops have catalogs of art and will order a selected print for a customer. Usually they are available in various sizes. If an old frame is utilized, glass which does not reflect is available, and the glass company will cut it to fit. After it is inserted, the picture, with or without matting, is put on. A heavy cardboard, perhaps retrieved from a corrugated box, is cut to fit the back opening, and brads are pounded in at intervals to hold it in place. In order to keep out dust and give a completed appearance, cut a piece of brown wrapping paper (or a heavy sack) to size, and cover the back opening. Affix it with brown masking tape in a continuous line around the frame. This acts as a seal.

When an antique chest, commode, or dresser is minus a mirror and one is considered desirable, it is possible to secure an old frame and have a glass company insert the looking glass in it. Currently, mirrors with a "distressed" appearance to establish a vintage feel are being sold at furniture stores which deal in new merchandise. Therefore, if you have a mirror which shows its age, you can consider yourself modish. However, some people do not appreciate wavy lines, distortions, or blotches. In large metropolitan areas it may be possible to have antique mirrors resilvered.

However, those who perform this task probably will not guarantee that breakage will not occur or that runs which can't be seen will not become evident when the stripping process is completed. Crating and freighting expenses are extra, so the cost can mount exceedingly. Bevelled edges and etching are not too commonly seen any more and may be considered desirable features to retain.

Chapter 12

WAS IT WORTH IT?

Well, was it worth it? Assess the answer yourself. When you acquire new articles from a furniture store, they achieve "secondhand" status as soon as they are in your home. Thus, their value is expected to descend. Not so with antiques. Everyone knows they've already been used, but, because they have that "something different" quality, they are not expected to decline but to increase in value. If you have taken a painted, shabby, discarded "in-the-rough" chest and restored it with a new finish, then you have raised its price tag.

Take black walnut. These trees are becoming so scarce that thieves are actually sneaking in to steal them from their owners' yards. Nowadays, when this wood is employed in furniture construction, it is customarily sliced as thin as $1/28''$ or $1/32''$ for the home market and $1/46''$ for export purposes. Its destiny is to become rich-appearing veneer over a base wood. Therefore, if you own a desk made out of solid inch-thick walnut, just think what value you have!

Antique furniture is considered a wise investment by Wall Street. After all, in 1971, United States citizens spent seven billion dollars on antiques and collectibles. Thus, it is to be anticipated that you can get your money back, and probably an additional bonus as well, from an antique for which you have paid a fair price.

There's also the creative urge and the let-me-do-it-by-myself desire to bring forth beauty which was not revealed before. The transformation from a cast-off to a crowning, conversational focal point for a room is possible when you repair and refinish an antique.

Naturally, you would expect to pay less for in-the-rough furniture or a blackened copper wash boiler which demand hours of labor to make them presentable, than for "mint condition" articles, already gleaming expensively in anticipation of their debut as coveted antiques. It's always fun to brag about a bargain and how hard you worked on the restoration when friends "Oh" and "Ah" over the result. If it's a family project, with husband and wife united as a craftsmanship duo or the offspring sanding ardently, the togetherness achieved does not bear a price tag. Consider, too, that working with your hands can be therapeutic, permitting you to take out frustrations on a battered box, instead of on family members or friends.

When your "new" old acquisition becomes a part of your decorating scheme, you have a touch that's your very own. In a development housing area, one woman may cover an empty tin can with string to make a planter. All up and down the street, other housewives copy the idea. Or a man may insert a set of windows in his front door, and facsimiles spread throughout the neighborhood. If you desire to be distinct in your decorating, antiques can be the answer, because no one else can find identical items with which to accessorize. Therefore, you have a personal atmosphere, and your home's personality is not a copy of the interior of every structure on the block. Are these pluses—initial low cost, augmented by investment potential; beauty; uniqueness; creativity; togetherness—powerful enough to entice you to acquire antiques and rehabilitate them? If so—good luck and happy stripping!